PALLBEARERS
ENVYING
THE ONE
WHO RIDES

BOOKS BY STEPHEN DOBYNS

PALLBEARERS ENVYING THE ONE WHO RIDES

STEPHEN DOBYNS

PENGUIN POETS

PENGUIN BOOKS

Published by the Penguin Group
Penguin Putnam Inc., 375 Hudson Street,
New York, New York 10014, U.S.A.
Penguin Books Ltd, 27 Wrights Lane,
London W8 5TZ, England
Penguin Books Australia Ltd, Ringwood,
Victoria, Australia
Penguin Books Canada Ltd, 10 Alcorn Avenue,
Toronto, Ontario, Canada M4V 3B2
Penguin Books (N.Z.) Ltd, 182–190 Wairau Road,
Auckland 10, New Zealand

Penguin Books Ltd, Registered Offices:
Harmondsworth, Middlesex, England

First published in Penguin Books 1999

1 3 5 7 9 10 8 6 4 2

LIBRARY OF CONGRESS CATALOGING IN PUBLICATION DATA
Dobyns, Stephen, 1941–
Pallbearers envying the one who rides: poems / by Stephen Dobyns.
p. cm.
ISBN 0 14 05.8916 3
I. Title.
PS3554.O2P35   1999
811'.54—dc21   99–18492

Printed in the United States of America
Set in Dante
Designed by Katy Riegel

For
Laure-Anne Bosselaar
and
Kurt Brown

CONTENTS

PART ONE: HEART I

PART TWO: OH, IMMOBILITY, DEATH'S VAST ASSOCIATE

PART THREE: HEART II

HEART I

∎

—Sir Bones: is stuffed,
de world, wif feeding girls.

"Dream Song 4"—John Berryman

■ ■ ■

keep looking at your clown's face in the mirror . . .

beware of dryness of heart love the morning spring
the bird with an unknown name the winter oak

"The Envoy of Mr. Cogito"—Zbigniew Herbert

■ ■ ■

Palmström schwankt als wie ein Zweig im Wind . . .
Als ihn Korf befragt, warum er schwanke,
meint er: weil ein lieblicher Gedanke,
wie ein Vogel, zärtlich und geschwind,
auf ein kleines ihn belastet habe—
schwanke er als wie ein Zweig im Wind,
schwingend noch von der willkommen Gabe . . .

"Gleichnis"—Christian Morgenstern

■ ■ ■

All winter long, it seemed, a darkening
Began.

"Robinson at Home"—Weldon Kees

GOOD DEEDS

Heart sits on a stump in the backyard,
dog turds, crusted snow lie all around.
A window opens, a voice shouts: Come
on back, Heart! But Heart won't budge.
You see, there is a dark place in the sky
despite the noon sun and lack of clouds.
A spot above the oak branch on the right,
like a dark splatter of spilled black paint.
If you stretched out your arm, your hand
could almost cover it. Heart can't explain it.
It feels like sadness but why is there sadness?
Heart sleeps okay, eats okay, moves his bowels just right.
It feels like despair but why is there despair?
Heart has pals, no big bills, and the roof doesn't leak.
As far as Heart can tell, life is going well.
The spot shimmers a bit and Heart thinks:
It's showing me that it knows I am here.
He imagines the dark spot leaving its home
in the morning—can sadness be pre-existing?
Could it fix like a tick on its victim's neck?
But perhaps this is someone else's sadness
and off on another street a gloomy stranger,
who feels often suicidal, feels okay today,
feels even optimistic. The oppressive weight
has not come back and he skips a few steps.
His sadness got lost, a not uncommon mistake.
Heart's muscular good cheer reasserts itself.
Although I feel terrible, he thinks, I don't really

feel terrible. I feel it for a stranger who today
gets a breather to let him rebuild a scrap of vigor.
Right now he feels down, but soon he'll come 'round.
Heart jumps from his stump. The day has just
begun but already he has done his good deed.
He'll eat a big breakfast, then make some calls.
In the evening may come a chance for Romance.
The black spot begins to fade. Soon it will be only
a pimple on Heaven's blue sky. Wasn't this inevitable?
The singing of formerly unheard birds grows audible.

THE HIMALAYAS WITHIN HIM

Heart worries about the sound of his own heartbeat.
If it must be percussive, why can't it be musical like
a steel drum or kettle? Or if not orchestral, at least
more aggressive like a dragon's bellow in a dark tunnel.
No one has yet critiqued the sound of his heartbeat.
Were they being polite? Did they discuss with one another
the puny patter of his inferior ticker? In Heart's
newfound chagrin, he wants to buy a megaphone
so his heart can boom, or a synthesizer so it can sing
like a Bach chorale. Timpanies, trumpets, tom-toms—
shouldn't his heart blare like a quartet of trombones
to declare his arrival? How lavish have been his loves—
shouldn't his heartbeat reflect his ardent complexity?
Instead it beats out a dull monotone: thump, thump.
But perhaps, thinks Heart, I delude myself. Perhaps
my passions are quite insignificant and my sensitivity
no greater than another's. Heart chuckles at the folly
of such a thought. Over the horizon lie the Himalayas
and within him rise his emotions, while the disparity
in elevation is slight. Heart decides that his sedate beat
is only camouflage. If it bespoke his feelings exactly
it would mean constant earthquake with people leaping
from skyscraper windows and babies yowling all night.
If it truly reflected the cataract within him, gladhanders
would nag him for favors. He'd waste his passion on trifles.
Once again Heart is struck by nature's immense cunning:
the complexity of the butterfly's wing, the salamander's
artful coloration, and his own heartbeat: constant and sly.

OLD WHAT'S-HIS-NAME

Heart writes a letter to the ones who are missing—
those who moved away or slipped through the cracks.
He wants them to know he misses them even yet.
Some go back to earliest childhood. What might
they look like? He realizes he must have passed
a few on the street without a flicker of recognition,
one with a cane, one with a beard, one with a red beret.
It's been a long time, he writes to the first.
Then he crosses it out. Many things have happened.
He crosses this out as well. How do you speak
to the disappeared? He remembers how some
made him laugh, some cry, some roll up his eyes.
He tries to recollect the smooth texture of their cheeks.
Those who died, how long have they lain in silence?
Those who live, do they stroll the streets even still?
His list contains several hundred names, other names
he can't recall. He sees their faces in the smoke.
He wishes he could clasp each one by the hand.
I wonder if you'll remember who I am, he writes.
Then he rubs it out. Recently I've thought of you.
He rubs this out, too. At last he hits on the right note,
which he prints on hundreds of cards. Some he inserts
in bottles he drops in the sea, some he ties to pigeons' legs,
most are swept up in the dry eye of a passing tornado.
Far away a bike messenger snatches a card from the air.
Still here, it says, followed by an indecipherable scrawl.
Old What's-His-Name, the fellow thinks: Up to his tricks.

LIKE A REVOLVING DOOR

Heart feels sad. He's tired of being a heart
and wants to be a lung. A lung never lacks
a sister or brother. He wants to be a finger.
A finger always has a family. Or a spleen
which only feels anger and is never sad.
Sometimes Heart feels joyous, beats with vigor.
But then the old stories resurface again:
hardship, cruelty, the Human Condition.
A kidney never faces these problems alone.
The eyes in unison devise a third dimension.
Not by being solo do the ears create stereo.
But Heart must turn outward for comradeship,
to seek another heart, a journey fraught
with uncertainty. Like a revolving door—
such is falling in and out of love. And
the betrayals! Heart needs only to consult
his book of broken hearts to feel pessimistic.
But soon he puts on a fresh shirt and heads out
to the highway. He hangs a red valentine heart
from a stick so people will guess his business.
No matter that the sun is sinking and storm-
clouds thicken. Approaching headlights glisten
on his newly pressed shirt and on his smile
which looks a trifle forced. Dust catches in his hair
and makes him cough. Why is Heart alone in the chest?

Because hope is an aspect of the single condition
and without hope, why move our feet? To see himself
as purely a fragment: such is Heart's obligation.
Let's quickly depart before we learn what happens.
Sometimes a car stops. Sometimes there is nothing.

FACING FAILURE

Heart lies on a board with his hands crossed
on his chest. He is neither resting, nor sick.
He's working very hard. His brow knots up
as he stares at the clock. Heart is investigating
the nature of boredom. I'm bored, I'm bored—
everyday he hears this said, both by people
he admires and by some he doesn't. Being a heart,
he has no chance for boredom. He is beating
every moment of the day and night. He pumps
blood and falls in love—these are his endeavors.
He thinks boredom is like being dead while still
having the benefits of life. You can eat a peach,
you can watch the sunset, you can walk the dog—
none of which will interfere with your suffering.
Boredom isn't like sleep since boredom isn't restful.
It isn't like meditation because the mind is blank
with a touch of complaint. Heart tries to lie very still.
Outside he hears a robin scolding his neighbor's cat.
He hears a buzz saw and the bouncing of a basketball.
Sunlight through the glass, the smell of cut grass—
Heart grows bored studying the nature of boredom.
I'm a total flop, he thinks. Surely, if he were smarter,
he could dig to the root of boredom and find a cure.
He imagines the glad cries of the afflicted. They would
lift him onto their backs and beg him to make a speech.
Wherever he went, he'd be pointed out as the person
who defeated boredom. Medals would coat his chest.

Heart slaps his forehead: again his mind has wandered.
He tries to face his failure. Like a sparrow I can't fly.
Like a monkey I can't swing from branch to branch.
Just getting through the day takes all his wits. He lacks
the knack to join the ranks of the ambulatory defunct.

GOODBYE TO THE HANDS THAT HAVE TOUCHED HIM

Rocky roads, sleepless nights, Heart decides
that love exists at the root of his problems.
Without love his path would be as smooth
as a plate of glass and he'd sleep like a kitten.
Without love, he could be a Brain. Wasn't it
only love that wouldn't let him think straight?
As a Brain, new work would stretch before him.
He could be a general and send troops into battle.
He could be a surgeon and cut hearts with impunity.
He could be a critic and dissect what he didn't like.
He would live in a stone house on a mountaintop.
New books of poems would be brought to him
and he would shout, No, no, no! He would eat
nothing but red meat. He wouldn't need friends.
He would be happy in the company of machines.
Then Heart wonders what do Brains do for fun?
For a Brain, a poem is just a collection of signifiers,
a sunset is just a sunset, a rose is only a color dying.
For fun, a Brain thinks solely about itself. Its house
has mirrors in place of windows. Every bed is soft.
Brain stands before a mirror and does the brain dance.
Instead of laughing, it grunts and rumbles. Instead
of singing, it coughs. Heart can't wait to get started.
But first he must say goodbye to his friends, those
who have hurt him, those who haven't hurt him yet.
He will bid farewell to all he loves: late afternoon light

upon the birch trees, goodbye to birds and bird dogs,
goodbye to the hands that have touched him.
This may take a few days but Heart won't dawdle.
No more resentment, no more sleepless nights.
He will toss out his emotions, chuck even his tear ducts.
One bright morning he will awake and be a Brain.
For breakfast he'll fry up a batch of dead poems.

THE NEW AUSTERITY

Heart is lonely so he buys a bird.
He lugs the bird all over in a silver cage.
In the morning, its feathers are orange,
in the evening aquamarine. He tells the bird
his life story, but when the bird stops singing,
Heart decides it's unhappy. He worries a bit,
then buys a cat to which he also tells his story.
At first the cat is cheerful, then it stops purring.
Heart thinks it's unhappy as well so he gets a dog—
nothing unique, just a mutt from the vet.
When Heart tells the dog his life story, the dog
starts to snore. It's more interested in the bird,
which feels drawn to the cat, which likes the dog.
Heart is pushed to the periphery of the relationship.
When he tries to speak, the others shush him.
When he walks around, they ask him to keep still.
Soon the bird, the cat, and the dog are laughing
and singing songs. But when Heart tries to sing
or tell a funny story, they ask him not to interrupt.
Heart makes their beds and carries out the trash.
The cat's fur gets all over the furniture.
The dog chews up shoes. The bird scatters seeds.
Heart is busy from sun-up to bedtime. He wonders
if he is still lonely, but loneliness is the luxury
of solitude and Heart has no time to spare.

Sometimes the cat pats his head, the bird sings him
a few notes, the dog scratches him under the chin.
At least, Heart tells himself, I'm being noticed.
In the new austerity of Heart's life, this is enough.

READY AND WAITING

Heart feels ready to begin the work of forgiveness.
The woman who jilted him; the man who tricked him.
Why tote these jagged rocks in his belly any longer?
He makes a list of his enemies: those who hurt him
on purpose; those who did it, so they said, by accident.
The list of names reaches the floor even when Heart
stands on a stool with his hands over his head. Such
is the extent of his sufferings. He'll absolve them all:
the man who mocked him, the woman who left him.
Heart writes down each incident. At times the old anger
begins to resurface. How could he stand such abuse?
But his mercy is like a spring breeze through pine boughs
and rancor skulks back to its cave. Briefly, Heart is happy,
but after forgiving his enemies, he needs to let them know.
He jots down a few words. His tone is gentle and benign.
Heart is struck by his own heart's capacity for goodness.
He seeks out each person who hurt him. He imagines
their delight when they get his note. Their nagging guilt
must have caused many sleepless nights. The first replies
begin to come in. Who did you say you were? asks one.
You have confused me with another, suggests a second.
Keep your forgiveness to yourself, says a third. Although
Heart also receives letters of appreciation and support,
his heart has room only for rude letters. He is shocked
by his mistake. If he hadn't forgiven his enemies earlier,
wasn't it because they weren't worthy of his generosity?
Having identified his tormentors, Heart feels almost content.

The trouble with forgiveness is that it leaves you defenseless. Heart builds a wall around his house. Motion detectors, steel shutters, hidden cameras—the next time, no matter what happens, nobody can say he was caught napping.

THE NATURE OF LOVE

Heart makes an inquiry into the nature of love.
First he picks out a pen, then he selects paper:
a journal bound in ostrich skin with rag stock.
Heart puts on soft music. He fixes the lamp.
Now he's ready to think about love. It isn't
like an onion, because onions make you cry.
It isn't like an eagle, because eagles fly away.
Heart's fallen in love over a thousand times.
He knows love like tightwads know gold coins.
It isn't like white cake, because cake turns stale.
It isn't like a rose, because roses shrivel and die.
The chair is soft, the room warm, and Heart soon
falls asleep. In a dream he hikes through a forest
until he finds Love sitting beside a tranquil pool.
Her diaphanous gown trembles in the breeze.
Her emerald-tipped slippers sparkle in the sun.
Heart sits at her feet as Love gives him a lecture
on the nature of love. Heart fills page after page
of his ostrich-skin book. He can barely keep up.
Back in the concrete world, the telephone rings.
It's the dentist reminding Heart of his check-up.
When Heart returns to his chair, his book is blank.
He vaguely recollects an amazing dream in which
the truth was made clear to him. Love, he writes,
is like a slipper with emeralds glittering on the toe.
Heart waits for more. In his mind's eye he can see
how the emeralds shone and their bright mystery
forms a window opening in the azure sky above him.

Soon from his pen precise words will spill forth.
He doesn't realize that wisdom has come and gone,
that he was out of the room when the answers
to his most pressing questions were made plain.
Soon Love will gallop up in her chariot and urge Heart
to climb aboard. He holds his pen aloft like a baton.

VALENTINE MATHEMATICS

Heart rides a wagon down a mountainside.
It bumps down, spins around, and nearly
kills him. When it comes to a stop, he drags it
back to the top and plummets down again.
Heart seeks metaphors for the nature of love.
One day he parachutes from a hot air balloon,
the next he sticks a pin into an electrical outlet.
He calls it his research. Always before he starts
he puts on a coat and tie. He brushes his hair
so it stays flat. Then he leaps in a bed of feathers
or smacks his head with a rubber mallet. Later
he writes his report which joins the others filling
the file cabinets in his bedroom. Heart believes
that love lies beyond his ability to understand,
which doesn't mean he won't try to figure it out.
So he soaks in hot water or puts a finger in a toaster.
If Heart were a stomach or lung, he would behave
contrarily but as a heart he has a certain obligation.
And love is so vast. Heart feels like a man preparing
to eat a hippo-sized turkey who begins by putting
a single feather on his lip. Despite decades of work,
Heart knows that he's only at the start of his labor.
He thinks when he's old and gray, at least a century,
he'll still be humming Schubert lieder and packing
his nose with pepper, then annotating the results.
But what about his answers? you ask. Isn't the world
crying out for his conclusions? Heart is perplexed

by the oddity of the question. His project is meant to fill the entire page of his life. His actions are like numbers in a column, under which Death will draw a black line. Those who come next can add them up.

LOVE IS ELSEWHERE

Heart journeys to a whorehouse to discuss love
with the ladies of temporary passion. The whores
are bored with his questions. Buy us a Coke, they beg.
Heart asks their secrets on the rhetoric of sentiment.
Is it their perfume or the way they toss their hair?
They sit on a couch as Heart paces back and forth.
Is it how you swing your hips or decorate your lips?
Three of the whores play pinochle, another naps.
Do you run Sunday specials, broadcast radio raffles?
Except the red light over the door, says the madam,
we have no need to advertise. Our product speaks
for itself. But where's love to be found? asks Heart.
The whores don't understand. I love my dog, says one.
I love my brother Mike, says another. A third plucks
a pubic hair and holds it aloft. Here's the distillation
of my devotion, she says. Soak it in milk for a week
and it grows as big as an alp. But Heart is discontent.
What about the emotional dimension of your work?
Sometimes I soothe their brows, says one. Sometimes
I sing a song, explains another. Then the madam
sees what Heart is after. You think we're a destination,
but we're a vehicle like any other. These girls are just
the machines men ride to get to a spot they never reach.
Our job is mechanical. Sex with us is like taking a bus.
As for love, we like to keep it out of the workplace.
The whores agree. I once found it at the beach, says one.
And I found it in the back seat of a car, says another.
But here? They shake their heads. The madam pushes

Heart toward the door. Write if you find it but don't
come back unless you mean to buy. By now it's late;
men line up out front. Some seem hopeful, others not.
Heart asks them where love may be found. The fellows
check their wallets. Not here, they say. One wiseacre
takes a buck and folds it so Washington appears to wink.
George has it, says the rascal, and as we're told in school
he cannot tell a lie. Nearby a night bird cracks a few notes
off-key—no doubt a smart alecky remark in bird talk.

BLACK STITCHES
DOWN THE MIDDLE

While Heart is at the butcher shop, a thief breaks
through his cellar window hoping to strike it rich.
Neatly folded on Heart's closet shelf, he discovers
stacks of rubber smiles from the comic to ironic.
He finds the false hands handed out up as hearty
handshakes, likewise splendidly coifed toupees,
eloquent speeches swearing gratitude or pleasure,
even an exquisite alabaster foot for when Heart
must put a best foot forward. The thief imagines
Heart to be a hypocrite of vast proportions. Where's
the authenticity in this fellow's life? Even criminals
fall prey to waves of indignation and this one decides
that Heart finds truth merely an option. But how unfair!
These are the tools Heart uses when he's feeling low,
those days when he's emotionally under the weather
and the dark pushes close. Better not leave the house
in such a funk, Heart thinks, so he picks the right smile
from his stack of smiles just as a banker chooses a tie.
When he's sad, Heart's handshake is humid and soft
so he selects a grip with muscle. When he's depressed,
his hair's a mess so he wears a wig with an exact part.
The world is jam-packed with comrades in misfortune
and Heart frets that his downhearted state will heighten
the level of their gloom. So he reconstructs himself
and departs his house a bewigged paragon of mirth.
But such intricacy of thought is lost on Heart's intruder

and, taking the garden shears, he hacks each smile to bits.
Now, on bad days, Heart goes out with a crooked smirk,
the result of a bunch of smiles patched back together,
as if he had flown through the glass of a pickup truck.
People jump when they see him, but the sad are made
no sadder and briefly they're distracted from their woe.
As for Heart, his oddity does double duty as he reaps
the rewards of his zigzag smiles and people's sympathy.

TROUBLE IN MIND

Blue shadows falling, Heart explains to the cat.
When it rains in here, it's storming on the sea,
he tells the dog. Heart feels blue. But this time
he's got it under control. For ten minutes a day
he wears glasses with blue lenses. Thus sadness
has its window of opportunity. For ten minutes
Heart lets sadness do its worst. Been down so long,
down don't worry me, he says, checking his watch.
It's like taking the dog for a walk—sadness gallops
through the backyards of Heart's interior, digging
holes and chasing cars until Heart whistles it back.
Without any bad luck, he says, taking off the glasses,
I'd have no luck at all. Heart feels better and sadness
feels better too, having stretched its muscles. Heart
puts on red glasses or purple, depending on his mood.
Should he sing or complain, crack jokes or write poetry?
But recently his sadness isn't happy with ten minutes.
It wants twenty or thirty. It demands the entire day.
It snatches the time Heart has set aside for joy or anger.
Heart removes his blue glasses but the world stays blue.
And if he tries to put on his yellow glasses for jealousy,
the world turns green with sudden envy. Heart wonders
if he wasn't wrong to let sadness toughen up. Instead
of being content, sadness wants to be boss, it wants
all the glasses blue. Heart sticks the glasses in a box
which he locks in a trunk which he hides in the closet.
Better let those sadness muscles turn to flab. Trouble
in mind, Heart thinks, but I refuse to feel blue always.

Putting on his red glasses, he waits for rapture to kick in. It's taking longer than usual. From the window Heart stares out at the autumn drizzle. Trucks grind their gears: salt trucks, dump trucks. But the streets outside are empty, slick with wet. These are the vehicles of Heart's interior. They shiver and drop gobs of oil. They rasp and growl.

WHY FOOL AROUND?

How smart is smart? thinks Heart. Is smart
what's in the brain or the size of the container?
What do I know about what I do not know?
Such thoughts soon send Heart back to school.
Metaphysics, biophysics, economics, and history—
Heart takes them all. His back develops a crick
from lugging fifty books. He stays in the library
till it shuts down at night. The purpose of life,
says a prof, is to expand your horizons. Another says
it's to shrink existence to manageable proportions.
In astronomy, Heart studies spots through a telescope.
In biology, he sees the same spots with a microscope.
Heart absorbs so much that his brain aches. No
ski weekends for him, no joining the bridge club.
Ideas are nuts to be cracked open, Heart thinks.
History's the story of snatch and grab, says a prof.
The record of mankind, says another, is a striving
for the light. But Heart is beginning to catch on:
If knowledge is noise to which meaning is given,
then the words used to label sundry facts are like
horns honking before a collision: more forewarning
than explanation. Then what meaning, asks Heart,
can be given to meaning? Life's a pearl, says a prof.
It's a grizzly bear, says another. Heart's conclusion
is that to define the world decreases its dimensions
while to name a thing creates a sense of possession.
Heart admires their intention but why fool around?
He picks up a pebble and states: The world is like

this rock. He puts it in his pocket for safe keeping.
Having settled at last the nature of learning, Heart
goes fishing. He leans back against an oak. The sun
toasts his feet. Heart feels the pebble in his pocket.
Its touch is like the comfort of money in the bank.
There are big ones to be caught, big ones to be eaten.
In morning light, trout swim within the tree's shadow.
Smart or stupid they circle the hook: their education.

WHAT GOOD IS LOVE UNLESS IT'S AGGRESSIVE?

Deck the halls with cock and balls, intones Heart
as he hangs strings of mistletoe across his ceiling,
despite the fact it's August and hot and the mistletoe
is made of plastic. But so what? Soon he calculates
that every square inch of floor space is over-hung
by the ceiling's carpet of green. Then Heart gets busy
on the telephone, calling every woman in his book.
As soon as his victim enters the room, Heart plans
to jump on her, then point upward if she complains.
Driven to it by convention, he'll maintain. Forced
against my best intentions to be bad. Heart is tired
of patiently waiting for the right girl to come along.
What good is love unless it's aggressive? he wonders.
These are just a few of the reasons he gives later
for why he flung himself on the gas meter reader,
a middle-aged shop steward with a bristly mustache.
Win some, lose some, thinks Heart. But just what
is he to do with his excess love? He pats every furry
creature he meets. He grins till his cheek muscles ache.
Yet ladies cross the street when they see him approach.
So Heart remains single as his heart bubbles and burns.
The air touching his skin pulsates with heat, cats scrap
for the right to sit on his lap. His pal Woody tells him,
I'll fix your problem. We need to put that juice to work.
Woody's a slumlord with ten blocks of cold-water flats.
He sticks Heart in the basement of a five-story walk-up

with a stack of dirty books. By now it's December and snow
heaps up in the parking lots. A tangle of tubing is hooked
to Heart's chest as he flips through lurid descriptions of smut:
Roman orgies, gruesome foursomes, pretzel gymnastics.
Up on the top floor an ancient codger bangs a hammer
on the radiator. Turn down the heat, he shouts, moments
before the greasy water in his fish tank breaks into a boil.

THE DARK AND TURBULENT SEA

Sailboat, sailboat—so Heart counts the ships at sea
in order to raise his thoughts above matters of flesh.
Heart is at the beach in his red swimsuit and nearby
on towels or tossing balls in the air are abundant
examples of female dazzle. Often Heart is comforted
by the waves' regulation, the distant line of watery
horizon, and the air with its mixed aspects of seafood,
salt, and sweat. But here at the beach Heart is no closer
to the sea's soothing sway and resultant philosophical
reflection than on a city street. Lolling and frolicking
nymphs, pink flesh, and half-bared breasts, consume
his vision and so in desperation Heart counts the ships
at sea—sailboat, sailboat—in hopes he'll be restored
to calm. This for Heart enacts life's essential problem—
the distant vista with its philosophical paraphernalia
is disturbingly hidden by the delights of the foreground.
Why, for instance, mull over his mortality when a bevy
of young ladies is engaged in a bosomy bout of volleyball
just a few feet away. Jiggle, jiggle, thinks Heart, it leads
to trouble. Sad to say, he hasn't thought of Kierkegaard
all day. Heart is even hesitant to swim or take a nap lest
he miss some beauty adjust a strap or hitch her halter up.
As for the dark and violent sea it's just a distraction, easily
ignored; moral issues, highbrow notions—all forgotten.
This is in answer to a question asked the next day by a man
in his car staring through his tempest-streaked windshield

at the wind-pummeled beach: Why's that guy sitting there
grinning? Heart's having a picnic, even though it's storming.
As he eats his carrot sticks and raindrops run down his neck,
Heart stares at the waves disappearing into the fog and feels
able at last to see what's there in peace. And what's that?
the man might ask. The usual mix: what lies ahead and what
has always been. All the immutable whys and wherefores.
But now Heart's distracted once again. Beneath the sand
he has found a polka-dotted bikini top. What amazing luck!
Heart presses it to his lips, then folds it neatly in his basket.
Is he aware of the wintry weather's fierce attack? Guess not.

FIGHTING BACK

At times it seems to Heart that the truck has left,
taking his friends to the beach while he remains behind.
This is the lackluster season of Heart's inertia, even
if sunny and warm. He tries to mow the lawn, eats soup
for lunch. It feels like his bones have tripled in weight
or a brick sport coat had been set on his shoulders. Hearing
a joke on TV, he says, Haha. But he says it modestly.
He says it because he thinks he should. Haha, he says
on the street. Haha, he says while walking in the park.
But he says it for practice, so his laugh won't get rusty.
These days it's hard to walk without his knees bent.
And his feet ache, as if gravity had become an enemy.
If he were pitched into the river, he'd sink like a rock.
But it's unlike Heart to be overthrown without a fight
and because he feels pushed down to earth he makes
himself a pair of boots with powerful coiled springs
attached to their soles. The more Heart is pressed flat,
the higher he bounces. If you stood on the next block,
you could see his passage down the street as his head
pops up above the roofline. Boing, boing—such is Heart's
locomotion. Dogs bark, children pursue him on bikes.
But, you ask, does he actually feel better? Perhaps not.
Heart thinks a diabolic brute is playing a funeral lament
on his soul's hurdy-gurdy, and therefore he feels weary.
But Heart hopes to outlast him. If not, he'll mock him
and bounce the best he can, even if it gives him a headache
and scares the birds. But if the struggle persists and at last
destroys him, then Heart will ask his heirs to put a jukebox

in his coffin to play band music twenty-four hours a day,
and folks passing the graveyard will feel a lightness of step
and even the conventional dead will gyrate their bones.
Oh yes, Heart has many such plans and his mind leaps
from one to the next as he stretches out on his couch
with a washcloth over his brow and the music turned low.

GREAT JOB

Heart considers the nature of fairness—
how some folks get pearls, others pebbles.
A rock falls out of the sky, who it smacks
is anyone's guess—butcher, crook, or priest.
Heart is struck by the unfairness of fairness.
What does it mean to deserve something?
A man works all day, then gets hit by a truck.
Another wins the lottery after robbing a bank.
Heart decides the concept of fairness is meant
to give shape to the shapelessness, suggesting
its reverse is not unfairness but the random,
which is there all the time. As for Civilization,
it's the confused attempt to impose structure
on randomness, or at least to drape the cloak
of causality around it, and so make it credible.
Heart begins to worry. He thinks Civilization
is losing the battle. Acts of unfairness appear
on the upswing. He glances out at the street.
It's raining; the wind is blowing. People bustle
along with heads bent as umbrellas go haywire.
Heart frets about wet socks and sore throats.
He hurries downstairs and out to the sidewalk.
Great job, he says to the first person he meets.
The man looks bewildered, then hastens away.
Heart keeps offering encouragement. Great job,
great job, he says to one and all. Are they pleased?
They think he's nuts. Nobody says thanks. Heart

stays out all day. He misses lunch. His feet hurt;
his throat aches. He thinks how soon he'll go home
and draw a hot bath. He'll splash about in the tub,
his nose poking above the bubbles, and never think
that he alone reaps the rewards of his manic guilt.

ONE GOOD TURNS
DESERVES ANOTHER

As a gift to his friends, Heart offers to take on
their burdens for a while. Each man and woman
bears a satchel of woe so Heart hires a wagon,
puts himself in harness, and drags it around
the track surrounding the local football field.
Some friends have more than one satchel.
They have big containers, they have a truckload.
But no matter. Heart hopes to give them a breather.
Load up, he shouts, as his friends stack suitcases,
packing crates, and steamer trunks onto the wagon
so it rises up a tottering alp of outrage, hardship,
and complaint—all the bad stuff. But for a bit
Heart wants to be accountable, he wants to do
his friends a good turn as he takes a few turns
around the track, leaning into the harness, sweating
like a pig even though it's winter and snowing
just a little. The tower of woe creaks and shifts.
Heart's friends dash off—some go dancing, others
hop in the sack. The straps bite Heart's shoulders,
his foot slips on the ice, and he nearly goes under.
While not happy, he's happy that his friends are happy.
He checks his watch. How long did he tell his chums
he'd help out? It's getting dark. Heart pulls his load
all night. Far away, he hears the whinny of laughter.
Once he spots a shadow running past. It looks like
his pal Woody, who gives a hasty wave. Dawn reddens

the eastern sky or is it his friends' party still going on?
One day leads to the next, one week leads to another.
As the weather changes, birds alight on Heart's cart
and construct their nests. From the top baby robins
test their wings. Far away Heart hears happy voices
raised in song. Spring turns to summer. And Heart's
own baggage of personal sorrow, where does it linger?
Heaped by the side of the track, his trunks wait their turn.
Heart had hoped that by accepting his present work he might
forget their plight. Tough luck. Meanwhile, Heart lugs
his freight. He focuses on his feet and tries to cheer up.
He needs to make the best of what looks like a mistake.
He begins to recite every bit of verse he knows by heart.

WHAT NEXT?

Heart tunes in his poetry shortwave crystal set.
His muse is transmitting him a message: tap, tap.
The Morse signal is never terribly clear. Is this
a communiqué about desire or pork belly futures?
Pig swill libido, Heart writes. That can't be correct.
Heart presses the antique headphones to his skull
so tight that he fears his ears will permanently dent.
Patiently, he waits. Now there's nothing but static.
Throughout the city famous poets in vine-covered
cottages crank up their machines and prepare to get
e-mail from the muse. Underlings pack their books
in crates, picked up by delivery trucks and hawked
at the crossroads of commerce and the arts. Drum
majorettes hand out prizes; marching bands abound.
Meanwhile, Heart believes he at last has a signal.
Bump, it says, bump, bump. In concentration, Heart's
brow resembles an old-time accordion as he strains
to hear what is no more than the beating of his heart.
Such disturbing music, he thinks. Between the thumps
he detects a darkness with perhaps a shade of purple.
He notices how the thumps give structure to the dark,
letting the signal provide the metaphysical parameters
of the transmission. He removes his earphones to listen.
Amid the tumult of the street, he hears a similar silence,
as if the day's clamor functioned to create an enclosure
for a tranquility that's always present. Heart thinks, Isn't
this the message of my art which tries to show mankind's
beginnings and what lies ahead? He ponders his poem.

Given the difficulty of his subject, he's sure the blank page
says it best, an expanse of white to demolish the reader
with metaphoric force: symbol of creation and destination,
a zero's vacancy which cacophony surrounds. It's done!
Now to give his work a title. "What Next?" he calls it.
He folds the sheet and mails it to a celebrated quarterly.
Should he double submit? Best not. He imagines an editor
opening the envelope. Surely his life will be transformed.
Heart prepares to greet his cheering flock. This time he swears
he won't wait around his front steps gawking at his mailbox.

CAN POETRY MATTER?

Heart feels the time has come to compose lyric poetry.
No more storytelling for him. Oh, Moon, Heart writes,
sad wafer of the heart's distress. And then: Oh, Moon,
bright cracker of the heart's pleasure. Which is it,
is the moon happy or sad, cracker or wafer? He looks
from the window but the night is overcast. Oh, Cloud,
he writes, moody veil of the Moon's distress. And then,
Oh, Cloud, sweet scarf of the Moon's repose. Once more
Heart asks, Are clouds kindly or a bother, is the moon sad
or at rest? He calls scientists who tell him that the moon
is a dead piece of rock. He calls astrologers. One says
the moon means water. Another that it signifies oblivion.
The girl next door says the Moon means love. The nut
up the block says it proves that Satan has us under his thumb.
Heart goes back to his notebooks. Oh, Moon, he writes,
confusing orb meaning one thing or another. Heart feels
that his words lack conviction. Then he hits on a solution.
Oh, Moon, immense hyena of introverted motorboat.
Oh, Moon, upside down lamppost of barbershop quartet.
Heart takes his lines to a critic who tells him that the poet
is recounting a time as a toddler when he saw his father
kissing the baby-sitter at the family's cottage on a lake.
Obviously, the poem explains the poet's fear of water.
Heart is ecstatic. He rushes home to continue writing.
Oh, Cloud, raccoon cadaver of colored crayon, angel spittle
recast as foggy euphoria. Heart is swept up by the passion
of composition. Freed from the responsibility of content,
no nuance of nonsense can be denied him. Soon his poems

appear everywhere, while the critic writes essays elucidating
Heart's meaning. Jointly they form a sausage factory of poetry:
Heart supplying the pig snouts and rectal tissue of language
which the critic encloses in a thin membrane of explication.
Lyric poetry means teamwork, thinks Heart: a hog farm,
corn field, and two old dobbins pulling a buckboard of song.

FLAWED LANGUAGE: THOUGHT'S SHADOW

Love letters, Heart is sick to death of love letters.
Maybe five a day flow from his pen. And this
for a nearly half a century. Heart calculates
he has signed his name to over fifty thousand
pledges of devotion and to how many women?
He can't begin to reckon. Yet solitude remains
his constant companion. Toddling off to bed
each night Heart is most often solo. His head
is the only one to touch the pillow. His toothbrush
alone adorns the sink. Perhaps there's a problem
with my syntax, Heart thinks, perhaps my diction
shows a lack of distinction. After such eloquence
he should be the Wordsworth of ardor, the Byron
of passionate expression, but this is not the case.
Good to hear from you, writes a lady in response.
Then nothing else. So sorry we can't do lunch,
says another. My nights are taken, writes a third.
Heart decides the fault must lie with the frailty
of language itself. His words reflect his emotions
as a toadstool stacks up against a redwood. No
wonder he's lonely. He can't shrink the contents
of his heart into a motley lot of nouns and verbs.
His romantic nature remains unfettered by grammar.
So he makes a special letter, a metallic billet-doux
which he designs in a buddy's blacksmith shop.
When done it weighs ten pounds. Heart ships it

to his current love, then he tidies up the house.
He puts champagne on ice and sits down to wait.
Soon he'll hear her little feet tripping up the stairs.
Sad to say his package gets waylaid. The post office
calls the police and Heart's love note lands in a field
surrounded by men in padded suits. X rays indicate
an infernal machine. The chief of police sets it off
as cops duck for cover. First erupts a blare of horns.
Then the sound of ripping paper as a mailed fist
on a steel coil slashes through the flimsy wrapping.
In the fist's grip is a steel gardenia which vibrates
at the pitch of angry honey bees. The cops retreat.
What next? But this completes Heart's nonverbal
billet-doux, apart from the words, *I love you*, cut
in italic on the knife-sharp petals of the metal posy.
A guillotine, thinks a cop. Man trap, thinks another.
That night Heart hears big feet rushing up the steps.
Has his stainless steel epistle truly worked so well?
Heart worries what to do with such hungry women.
Is he, in fact, sufficiently masculine? So he thinks just
before the cops bust down the door and drag him to jail.
Court suits and legal costs proliferate. Defeated again,
Heart returns to common diction for his lovelorn fiction.

LUMBERJACK SHIRTS AND MOTORCYCLE BOOTS

Lacking muscles that pop from beneath his shirt,
Heart asks whether he is masculine enough. True,
he owns no princess phone and the color pink
is absent from his closet apart from a pair of socks,
which, anyway, were a gift, but should he beef up?
Cart his violets and gardenias to the compost heap?
Transport those thin volumes of verse to the dump?
If the masculine is a scale, then where should Heart
put his mark? Down near the bottom or at the top?
Wouldn't he do better if he cultivated more muscle,
replaced his college button-downs and penny loafers
with lumberjack shirts and motorcycle boots? Heart
strokes his cheek. Wouldn't it help to grow a beard
and learn to hunt, ransack the forest with a black
powder musket in search of a Bambi for his lunch?
Or sports. Heart pictures his team down by three points
as he gets up to bat. Wouldn't a grand slam be worth a date?
What does it mean to be a man? Lacking a bosom
is at least a start—physically Heart has got it right
and, even with parts lopped off or swapped, a mother
he would never make. Isn't manhood more than cock
and balls? Shouldn't Heart expand his range of insults,
flatten a ruffian, hawk, spit, and pump his muscles up?
In a wig shop Heart discovers a toupee of chest hair.
Though Heart has adequate fleece above his heart
he decides a new nipple carpet is what he needs—

a bristling thatch of multicolored strands. He calls the clerk and shortly Heart has the counter strewn with chest wigs—black, blond, red, and brown. But would it be sufficient to attach them to his exterior? I'll take ten, says Heart. The clerk nods. Gift boxed? he asks. No, no, declares Heart, I'll eat them here.

I'M MUSCLE, I'M BRAWN

Hearing the pet shop has picked up a load of pups,
Heart hastens to check them out, but as he crosses
the street a brick drops from an iffy cornice. Ouch!
Heart wakes up in a hospital. The doc sticks a mirror
in his face. Who the heck is that? demands Heart.
He doesn't recognize himself. What a dope, he thinks.
Your papers say you're Heart, the doctor explains.
Not me, Heart protests, I'm muscle, I'm brawn.
Let me out of here. He plucks off the bandage,
knocks the doc to the floor. Close call, he thinks.
To celebrate, he swipes a cherry-colored convertible—
the back he packs with booze, the front with girls.
Let's get some speed out of this crate, he shouts.
He steers with his knees with two girls on his lap.
Between kisses, he sings. When not singing, he drinks.
He chucks the empties so they break in the street.
Who are you, big guy? asks one girl. I'm muscle,
boasts Heart, I'm brawn. He aims for dogs and cats.
He swerves at old folks just to watch them jump.
He drives through front yards, backyards, graveyards—
it's all the same to Heart. His job is to have fun.
Before long the cops are chasing him all over town.
Heart can't hear the radio because of the sirens.
He can't enjoy the kisses because of the bumps.
He flings whiskey bottles back at the cop cars.
When the cops begin to shoot, the girls bail out.
Soon the booze is gone. A cop's lucky shot clips
the visor which snaps off and strikes Heart smack

in the noggin. He goes out like a light. His car
bumps against a hedge and the cops drag him out.
He wakes up in the hospital where the doc sticks
a mirror in his face. That's me all right, says Heart.
The cops and doctors cluster together to decide
Heart's fate. It's jail or the hatch for this nutcase.
When they turn their backs, Heart sneaks away.
The sun's low in the west. The day has gotten late.
His only wish is to see the pups before they're sold.
On the street, people leap from his path, others yelp.
Heart doesn't realize that these are the folks he nearly
crushed an hour ago. He thinks they're being polite.
Heart is touched. He considers the human condition—
how courtesy and compassion go right to the bottom.
In the pet shop window, ten pups nip each others' ears.
They growl and tussle. They look brutal but Heart sees
it's play. People dodge past him. Does he pay attention?
Perhaps not. Heart burps and pats his lips. How strange
that whiskey's smoky tang should overwhelm his tongue.

ADRIFT IN THE
LEAFY TRANQUILLITY

After a dragon has been seen in the neighborhood,
making cows curdle their milk and scaring sheep,
Heart decides to investigate. He constructs armor
from old fenders, rents a horse from a riding school,
and equips himself with sword and shield. The dragon
isn't hard to spot. Its fiery breath leaves a telltale haze.
I guess I'm your captive, says the dragon. Heart asks,
Don't you want to fight? Why bother? says the creature.
I'm sick to death of the forest with its rain and sleet.
So Heart invites it home. It won't stay in the barn
because of the cold. It won't sleep in the basement
because of the damp. Heart makes a bed in the den.
The dragon's spikes tear the sheets. Its fiery breath
leaves soot marks on the ceiling. At Heart's bedtime,
the dragon wants to talk. Have you ever wondered,
it asks, why we were put here on this earth? Please,
begs Heart, not tonight. But the dragon wants to tell
its life story, what it was like as an egg and its years
as a lizard. Whenever Heart nods off, the dragon
pokes him with a claw. My mother thought me ugly.
My father ran off when I was two. I'd like to have
a wife and kids and settle down. Is that a lot to ask?
But Heart seems fast asleep. Soon the sun comes up.
The dragon fries a dozen eggs and leaves the plates for Heart.
It's eager for his friend to wake so they can discuss
the meaning of life, the national debt, and where flies go

in winter. It wanders through the house, proclaiming
and gesticulating, while Heart pretends to slumber.
It had seemed so simple—an evil in the forest which
Heart could overcome. He hears the dragon ramble on
about how every living creature has a need for friends.
Heart begins to yearn for the restful vacancy of the forest.
Couldn't he disguise his looks and take the dragon's place?
Maybe he could find serenity within the leafy tranquillity.
If he grew bored, he could chase cattle, eat some sheep.
And when at last a champion rode forward to slay him,
he would meet his fate boldly and keep his mouth shut.

TO CONCEAL
THE PIERCING LIGHT

For a few weeks Heart lugs about an antique possum
by the name of Mike. Piss-poor, piss-ugly, pissed-off,
and incontinent to boot, Mike is for Heart a study
in humility, which Heart thinks he needs. To himself
Hearts says, You are too vain, too proud, too arrogant.
So he carts Mike in a cardboard box hoping that a bit
of Mike's insignificance will stick to him. The possum
stumbles over his feet and spills his food. I need this,
Heart concludes, I need to give up my shortcomings.
He thinks when he's truly humble he'll wear only white.
He will walk with a cane even if he doesn't need one.
He will speak so softly people will say, What? Say what?
He'll eat only nuts. He practices the phrase, But tell me
what *you* would like. He waits for Mike's direction.
But Mike is unable to accept the gravity of his mission.
He fights the dog and raids the trash for juicy scraps.
Instead of playing dead, he strops the tips of his claws.
He wants to go back to the forest to fornicate and hunt.
You're too decrepit, shouts Heart. But Mike disagrees.
With his remaining teeth, he snaps at Heart's fingers.
So Heart takes him back to the woods and sets him free.
Mike shuffles off between the oaks to seek his last battle
and to make a meal for crows. He won't even say thanks.
The mistake, Heart decides, was to try to take my lesson
from any living thing. He crouches before the doormat.
Tell me what life is all about, he asks. But the doormat

lies there sullenly until Heart gives it a kick. Sorry, sorry,
says Heart, feeling contrite. Perhaps humility, he thinks,
trying once again, means concealing the piercing light
of one's being. It's not that Heart can shine any less,
he can only make his shine less bothersome to others,
which implies humility isn't a matter of vision but display.
Heart buys a big hat. He carries an umbrella in all weather.
Isn't humility just a form of silence? To pass through life
like one on a secret errand, that's Heart's new obligation.
Heart puts a finger to his lips. Meanwhile his mind races.

OCCUPANT IN
PERMANENT TRANSIT

Heart brings back a hermit crab from the beach
and puts it on a roller skate with a midget motor
which the crab can work by the subtle direction
of its antenna-like stalks. You see, Heart wants
to pin down the exact definition of Home. Heart
lacks one, or so he thinks. True, he owns a pillow
and a bed to go with it. True, he has a place to hang
his lunch box, but is this home? Heart, it seems,
was born on the fly. Gypsies his parents weren't
but for all the home Heart's got, they might as well
have been vaudevillians frolicking the dusty burgs
till Heart was popped from a type of Saratoga trunk,
which has brought him to his current labor. Isn't
a hermit crab a creature with a house on its back?
How could the crab feel lonely if where it stood
was where it had to be? Never homesick or lost.
It just packs up its roots and trundles ahead: past,
present, and future in a single box. As for Heart,
when asked about his habitat, he waves vaguely
at his country's map, then adds, But only recently.
Checking his family tree he finds an accumulation
of forwarding addresses, going back to a note tacked
to the front gate of the Garden of Eden: Occupant
in Permanent Transit. That's me, concludes Heart.
Such negative thoughts have led Heart to the purchase
of crab, roller skate, etc. On the floor of Heart's room

the crab directs its skate in supple circles: a waltz sans
Strauss and violins. No noise but the hum of wheels.
The crab's snoot juts from its front door. Heart stares
until his eyeballs ache. Can't I make my life like this?
Neat trick. Transition, transition—Heart sees mortality
as trajectory, soaring through the air in a lugubrious arc
from inception to conclusion. Instead, he would prefer
a cushy chair in which to lounge during life's brief flight
and a second so he can bring a chum when he gets glum.
He wants a shell like the crab's but with room for a pal,
something like a house; or bigger, a stadium so he can
invite all his friends; even bigger, a crab with a basket
as big as Alaska on its back. Bigger yet, the very planet.

TO SLEEP THE SLEEP
OF THE JUST

Heart is visited by the police who want him to discuss
his neighbor who's been printing C-notes in his cellar.
Heart is troubled. Though he knows nothing, he thinks
he should keep his trap shut. So he pretends to know
a lot. With his eyebrows, he indicates, What I could
tell you if I chose. With his frown, he suggests, You'll
have to twist my arm to find out. What is important
is the expression of solidarity with a fellow sufferer.
The fact that he might be a crook is beside the point.
Of course the police know that Heart knows nothing.
Their questions are merely a formality. And Heart has
never actually met his neighbor, though he's seen him
mowing the lawn. So from the start Heart and the cops
are locked in an ethical struggle. The police can't permit
Heart to keep silent and Heart can't let himself speak.
Even though the morning is warm and birds are singing,
the cops could be torturing Heart in an ogre's chamber.
Only the screams are missing, only the physical suffering.
Heart clamps his jaw shut; the cops elevate their fists.
Their facial expressions are all over the emotional map.
But let's get past the threats and Heart's defiant shrugs.
Soon the moral high ground has become a muddy swamp
and the police haul Heart off to jail. He feels like St. Joan,
the cops feel like General Patton. Meanwhile the neighbor
returns home. He makes a sandwich, he kicks the dog.
He is as frail a reed as any citizen with a mother he loves

and friends he knocks about. But for Heart it's sufficient
that he breathes. Let others judge him. Heart is defending
a principle. Though by midnight in a jail cell the principle
burns dim as he tosses and turns on naked springs. Heart
has read that the Just sleep soundly, but he can't drift off.
He counts aloud as troops of shaggy Socrates hop fences.
Just the fear the old fossil might fall flat keeps him alert.

WOUNDS WITHOUT PAIN

For Heart this earth is neither spherical nor flat.
One day it's a rhomboid, the next it's pretzel-shaped.
How else to account for people's shifting moods?
One man is sluggish, another jumps up and down.
A day later their roles are reversed. And Heart too—
one day mad, one day glad, the next hopeful, the next sad.
Isn't this proof of the planet's physical vicissitudes,
the pressure of mountain ranges upon the atmosphere,
making the air weigh more in Montana than Vermont,
so even the ocean takes up less space and fish go crazy?
Troposphere, biosphere, stratosphere—and worse,
it happens at sixty thousand miles per hour as we rush
through space. Heart decides to correct these defects
with the use of an atmospheric suit of his own design.
Presto, the suit adapts itself to reflect barometric shifts,
electromagnetic fluctuations, and the earth's alterations
from triangle to cone. With it on, Heart feels instant calm.
The completed suit approximates a deep sea diving suit
which Heart makes cheap so each atmospheric sufferer
can fix his gravitational complaints. But nobody buys.
Let choose between fashion and serenity, people pick looks.
Heart wears his suit each day. In his mood of amiable
tranquillity, the rude stares of passersby don't touch him,
nor does anything else. A friend slaps him on the back;
it feels as light as a raindrop. Outside his faceplate Heart
contemplates the raging tempests of human emotion.
Inside he's cozy, if a little bored. Soon he gets lonesome.
He misses the hearty handshakes and affectionate pats.

He frets about people being downhearted without him.
Because of his constant calm, he feels constantly drowsy.
He has no need for fun, hears no music, eats only the basics.
Loneliness without sadness is like a wound without pain.
Is he feeling things without knowing he is feeling them?
What pleasure is he missing, what's his sorrow all about?
At last Heart can tolerate these perplexities no longer
and he runs out to the street without his protective suit.
His friends hurry forward to embrace him. Once again
Heart climbs aboard the emotional roller coaster. Never
has he been so uplifted, never has he been so cast down.
Arm and arm with his chums he hastens toward his end.
Only rocks stay put, he thinks, folks like us live on the fly.

THUS HE ENDURED

Heart's friend Greasy gets nixed by a stroke.
His pals give him a wake; they drink all night.
The next day they cart the coffin to the church.
In life, Greasy waxed cars; now he's defunct.
The priest says how Greasy's in a better place.
Heart takes exception. What could beat this?
Some mourners weep; others scratch their butts.
In life, Greasy was a practical joker. Even salt
in the sugar bowl wasn't too childish for him.
When the service is over, Heart and five friends
heave the coffin on top of their shoulders.
Outside it's raining. They wait for the hearse.
Maybe it's late, maybe it showed up and left.
The priest locks the church. The last cars depart.
Let's carry the coffin, it's just a few blocks.
As they set off, Heart hears a whistle. Show some
respect, he complains to a buddy in back.
In life, Greasy often asked, What's the point
and What comes next? Heart thought his jokes
helped keep the dark at arm's length. Rain drips
down the pallbearer's necks. Because of the fog
they can't see beyond their noses. Right or left?
If their hands weren't full, they would flip a coin.
Someone plays the harmonica, then starts to sing.
The pallbearers look at each other, it's none of them.
In life, Greasy reached three score years and ten.
He had a wife, four sons, and five Great Danes,
but not all at once. He always drove a Chevrolet.

Did we take a wrong turn? asks Heart. The rain
turns to sleet; it's getting dark. Someone starts
playing the trombone. A tune both melancholy
and upbeat. Where could it be coming from?
In life, Greasy felt a lack. He worked too hard,
the holidays were short. His wife kept asking
why didn't he do better? Then his sons left home.
Greasy stuck rubber dog messes on the hoods
of his friends' cars. This is what life's all about,
he'd think. Thus he endured. It begins to snow.
Heart shoulders his load. The sun goes down.
Will Greasy get planted today? It looks unlikely.
Heart watches the road. He can't see that the coffin lid
is tilted up and Greasy perches on top, just a shadow
of his former self. With both hands he flings wads
of confetti. He's a skeleton already. Heart would
scratch his head but he'd hate to let his corner drop,
his pals ditto: pallbearers envying the one who rides.

PART TWO

OH, IMMOBILITY, DEATH'S VAST ASSOCIATE

———————————■———————————

(OH, IMMOBILITY,
DEATH'S VAST ASSOCIATE)

Oh, immobility, death's vast associate,
you are the still center around which we jog.
Could you be more than idea? Even a grave
is mounted on the earth, which rolls around
the sun, which tumbles through the galaxy,
but here my astronomy fails me. A black hole
or the moment preceding the Big Bang;
an inwardness, a slumbering. But do you see
how nothing immobile could truly exist?
Yet at times in the morning upon waking
I have felt this immobility, something
holding me down: a grand disinclination.
You know how it is? Once the foot hits
the floor, there'll be no rest till bedtime.
Better not start. Better remain inert.
Immobility: you might think it the size
of the tomb. You are wrong. It's more gigantic
than New Jersey: a state dented by traffic,
a battered rectangle. I was born there.
Is this what I feel in the morning: the state
of my birth jammed in my gut? New Jersey:
locus of automotive fracas. No wonder
I can't get started. Do others have their
home states snagged in their bellies? Is this
a universal complaint? It grew in the night
and now they sit on their beds with their feet

on the rug and can't advance. All that weight:
Texas longhorns, Florida swamps. Who can doubt
they need more sleep. I need to rest, they say,
meaning a delay, a vast procrastination.

■ ■ ■

Perhaps you have felt this in the morning, a great
aloneness, as if life were fixing your blindfold
and her dark partners were raising their rifles.
Isn't this when the faces of our enemies show up
with their meaty smiles, while our friends are out
buying straw hats with blue ribbons, high-fiber
dog food, whistles? They scratch their heads.
They are distracted just when we need them most.
And we would call to them but something has gripped
the tips of our tongues. And we would run, but we
wear bronze slippers and our knees no longer bend.
Am I turning into a statue? we ask. Am I becoming
part of a wall? Yet around us six billion people
are engaged with their day. They begin just beyond
the bedroom door. How could one possibly feel alone
in their company? Tell me, could a brick in a wall
ever feel isolation? Or a drop of water in a pond?

■ ■ ■

At any moment on the planet, buckets of sperm
are being propelled forward, enough excrement
is cascading downward to pack a Mack truck.
Freeze this moment and a million morsels
are frozen on their journey to the tongue
as thousands of the sated suck their teeth.
Scratch your balls and five hundred others

duplicate your gesture. Groan, cough, fart,
sing—you are not alone. Are you worried?
Millions are worried. Are you happy? Millions
laugh with you. Or you sit in a corner moaning,
I am so sadly solo! In a thousand corners,
kindred notions plague your brothers and sisters.
To divide these sufferers across the entire day
means seventy thousand souls for every second.
Their joined sighs would overwhelm the thunder.
Burps, trips, flops, sleeps, hopes, slips:
you get the point. So let's return to the problem.
Do you think no one understands you? Do you find
only an indentation in the depths of heaven?
Shrug your shoulders, throw up your hands, say,
What's the use? At this second the same words
are being spoken in Urdu, Farsi, and Dutch.
Robbed of aloneness and particularity, we feel
most human in aloneness and particularity.
Even as I write these words, a solitary Pakistani
is penning a poem on similar themes, though his
of course is no match for mine. What is this
barrier in the brain that believes nothing exists
on the other side? What point does it serve? If,
like a turtle's shell, it's meant to be protective,
how am I kept safe by the illusion of isolation?

■ ■ ■

Consider, for instance, the ants: don't they
jointly make a mental puddle, as if the colony
together composed a single brain? Consequently,
each ant forms only a fragment. This one represents
part of a vague feeling of dislike, and here

is a smidgen of hunger or love or laughter.
Ten at once produce a thought, one hundred create
an elemental philosophic question, like, what
is the excuse for this lonesome antheap anyway?
Possibly we humans perform a similar function
and six billion make up your basic cerebrum. This
must be why the earth is round and head-shaped:
a single cranium swirling through the void, trying
to articulate the answer to Why and Why not, trying
to work out the conundrum of its creation and why
anything should happen next. So when you feel lonely,
it only means you are not being thought of at this
particular moment. Your turn will come tomorrow
or next week. You are a gray cell used primarily
to investigate the metaphysical and today the brain
as a whole has turned its attention to pleasure,
which is why your neighbors are having so much fun,
but soon the brain will shift to gloomy thoughts
and at that time you will be called upon again.
Immobility, then, is just a time out period,
a chance to recover one's vigor, before one takes
one's place in the vast articulation of Why Bother.
How *could* a brick in a brick wall ever feel lonely,
or a grain of sand within the Sahara? Clearly
you are wrong to feel this emotional dislocation.

■ ■ ■

A library is a spot where outworn reasons may relax,
and big ones contain more antique thought than most.
That furry Neanderthal or early Cro-Magnon doodling
with charcoal an animal's shape on the cavern wall
was articulating an answer to the question of Why.

fabric of skin and fabric of home grown to be one,
brains become the mental ditto marks of deck chairs?
And consider. Your time is already allotted: running
or standing still lasts just as long. You might argue
that a boring life has twice the length. Yet by being
cozy with the immobile, have you really lived at all?
Haven't you become no more than death's inert buddy?
You have lasted by not calling attention to yourself.
You regularly moved your bowels, making compost,
returning earth to earth: you even voted Republican!
You were immobile in your mobile home. You breathed
but not too much. Only your sperm moved fast;
only your monthly blood came in a gush. For the rest,
you followed directions, you did as you were told.
I cannot tell you how much the earth respects you.
Here, take this prize, a little golden tombstone
to pin to your heart. In your next life, should you
be so lucky, you will return as grass, even macadam.

■ ■ ■

I think the color of immobility must be black,
not brown or almost black but a complete lack
of color, a vacancy of color. And it is quiet,
a vacancy of sound. If it had a taste that taste
would be as bitter as bile, and if it had a smell
it would be the hint of something metallic
like a rusty tire iron or hubcap, and its touch
would be wintry. What is the taste of Why bother?
What is the color of not desiring or dragging
the feet forward, what is the smell of surrender?
The space it occupies is the space within a zero.

The light it sheds is the overcast twilight
of a winter evening. And if it had a time, the two
hands of its clock would be always pointing up.

∎ ∎ ∎

Further examples: the rich desire the poor to be passive.
The teacher wants his students subdued. The shopkeeper
wishes his shoppers submissive. The man wants his wife
to be compliant. The mother wishes her children docile.
The government wants the electorate to be somnolent.
The cop wishes the crooks to be inactive. The housewife
wants her husband to be constant. The poor wish the rich
to be yielding. The voters want the government quiescent.
The crooks wish the cops to be inert. The students
want their teacher nonresistant. Each person hopes
his neighbor will be unassertive. You see how it works?
Immobility, our vast enemy, the quality we urge on others.

∎ ∎ ∎

The house of pleasure keeps its windows painted black.
A red light above the door and we enter. Fuck all night,
bugaloo all day: every orifice has its form of having fun.
Bang, bang, who knows what's happening on the street?
Have another morsel, another polka, another bottle,
another smooch. His stiff prick taught him the Letter I
and the Number One. Onward, brave, little soldier!
Let's deflower the moment by embracing the carnal.
Is there any better method of dismantling the clocks?
This isn't quite mobility, nor is it standing still. Do you
envy the ones whose hearts popped when their pricks
were playing piston? At least they never had to wake up.

And isn't that the point? What happens when you reenter
the boulevards, when you rejoin the gray light of day?
Bald already? What a pity. Need a walker, need a cane?
I too like my memories but their caloric content is nil.
Whoever got fat eating the past? Distraction is only
a form of inaction, eyes shut tight against the dark.
Then what? To sit and rock and stare out at the street?
To lie in your coffin encased in postcoital triste?

■ ■ ■

Possibly immobility is the recognition of isolation.
Press your hand to the hand of your favorite love
and you still have two hands. Your words in another's
mouth are no longer your words. With my prick I enter
my dearest only briefly, then I forget, go off to eat
French toast or study the sunset. One hundred thousand
happy fans cheering a soccer play—a kick, a pass,
a goal—don't they cheer one hundred thousand plays?
Yet never disheartened we pursue the dream of connection.
A man or woman spots a suit in an upscale shop and thinks
I'd look good in that. That bowler hat would set me off.
That blouse will make me shine. Each bizarre garment
you see worn by some hopeful applicant on the street
is the result of such judgment. I'd look great in that.
Meaning, of course, this will make them like me more.
The stories we collect, the shoes we wear, the smiles
we try out in the mirror are all assaults on the barrier.
I will make of myself a rocket in order to pass over!
I will be a locomotive and smack that wall extra sharp!
I'm exhausted by living in my own private birdcage!
So we incite ourselves and bluster and leap about.

And the result of this stubborn combat with isolation?
Press your palm to another, there remains a division.

■ ■ ■

Each dance step we execute is a slap in the face
of immobility. Are you light on your feet? Do you wear
tap shoes and feel an elasticity of sole and thus
you spring upward? What makes this more than
merely bouncing? Because you seek a chosen path.
Some tunes jingle inside, some tunes jingle outside.
This is when the extremities recall having been wings,
when the blue sky bends down to help us heavenward.
Just yesterday you weighed three hundred pounds and
now you're a feather rising on the notes of somebody's
whistling. What is music anyway? ask the scientists.
Being limited by what they know, they turn to math.
It must be counting, it must be numbers, it must be time.
And what is music's opposite? Silence? Almost correct.
Music's opposite is the tomb and so we dance to keep
the shadows back if only from the heart's dark corners.
The grave cannot stand a racket and even a tapped foot
is a form of boogie. You call it time? It is forever.
To spin on the pinnacle of one's genitals. To kiss
gravity goodbye. To bear the souls of birds in the belly,
as harmonies loop and dip behind your eyes. This one
likes Bach, this one Bop, this one likes the Beatles:
and so their feet are carried aloft, lungs throb and
palpitate, the pores pour forth their cheery tears
of pleasure. Even the skeleton chants a creaky song.
And immobility? It only has to wait. What is age but
the process of bringing the dancing inward? The heart

opens and two by two the dancing feet pass through:
an ark sailing the body's blessed blood to the grave.
You had your battle, little soldier. You danced a lifetime.
Those stones and monuments, those memorials and tombs:
without their weight the ground would hop. Oh, immobility!

■ ■ ■

A man in his rocker in the evening whistles a tune.
Warm breezes waft through the open window. Outside,
a dog barks. The man thinks of his past, considers
the future, thinks of his supper. Slowly, a skeletal
hand slides over the window sill, bridges open space,
and, poke, flicks the man on the back of his neck.
Man leaps, tables fall, cat runs up the curtains.
Immobility hates to jump. Why is a punch line called
a punch line? What is a joke but a poke in the neck?
Immobility shudders as the imagined straight line veers left.
Isn't the unexpected only a dip in the road, a sudden
collision to deposit you not in a gully but perhaps
in Akron, Tucson, Kansas City? Did you hear the one
about the terrorist poet who tried to blow up a bus
but burned his lips on the exhaust pipe? Chuckle,
chuckle. And all that is immobile gets a little slap.
A joke is an escape hatch from the nose-diving second.
We may not take it, but we like to know it's there.
How carefully we make our plans, yet how we delight
in the unexpected. Let's say your life unfolds more
or less according to your map. Where do you end up?
Immobility. Consequently, you buy lottery tickets,
hit the track, deal out a deck of cards, even sex
makes one yell and leap about, within the genitals,

within the heart. A joke spins you to the left,
a fright to the right. Both give the immobile a kick.
But slapstick only works when someone else goes splat;
when it happens to you, it's sad. How complicated
become our desires: to be surprised but not too much;
to be taken unawares but not to be taken too far.
And the fear? The hallway without an end; the horror
around the corner; joke turned to anarchy; music
to cacophony; no shut door to bring it to a close. You see?
The immoderate and the immobile are equally nasty.

■ ■ ■

Six acrobats teeter on one another's shoulders,
while the one on top juggles ten china plates:
so they give a smack to the face of gravity
and we are pleased. Does this mean we despise
gravity? Far from it. Who wants to be a helium
balloon rubbing the gloomy underbelly of clouds?
Or sad, shadowy sparks shot into outer space?
So does art mock all that is immobile and yet
it requires a frame, which is immobility itself:
just as sleep surrounds our diurnal endeavors,
so repose enwraps a poem and quiet encloses music.
Where would we be if the book lacked a binding
and the pages flew like birds about the room?
Within any painting exist assorted options
of motion. Gravity is beaten, death sent packing,
immobility overcome, but only for a jiffy. Yet
inside us too it is defeated for a while. Our focus
has been diverted from the linearity of our path
and briefly we are awash in virgin horizons—aren't
ten million alternatives begging to embrace us?—

then we sigh, shoulder our pack, and trudge forward.
In such a way will night create a lustrous sunset
to alleviate the dark, even though in memory only.

■ ■ ■

Perhaps the Capitalists are right after all. The best
distraction is a life rich with accumulation. But the sum
of ten cars is still ten cars. What's the sum of ten sunsets?
What's the sum of love? Not just sexual, though that
of course plays a big part. Paternal, fraternal, even
to have taught some brat to like Mozart is sweet.
But then we detect hordes of dislikes: the geezer
on the street who cut me off in his Cadillac? Can I
love him? The old fart? I'm just not that good yet.
Maybe I'll toss him a posy when he tumbles to hell.
Still, the immobile must hate all that loves, not
just the distraction, but the affirmation of motion.
Bach leapt into a cantata and so he escaped death.
Dear old Yeats became a singing bird. This is not
a new argument. Are there new arguments to be had?
Do you need something new or something convincing?
If the sum of a person is greater than his parts,
then someone may be the portion of a greater sum.
Grind away, grind away. I got my eye on an answer.
If to move means existing as a fragment of motion,
then immobility, like a corpse, is complete in itself.
Can you give fifteen good reasons for breathing?
Are you too busy living to surrender? Immobility
suspects it can wait. Patience is what it's best at.
You think you own today; it's got its paw on tomorrow.

■ ■ ■

Were immobility a soldier, entropy would be its rifle.
Heat cools, activity slows, molecules adulterate:
the Second Law of Thermodynamics is God's response
to the Big Bang. I think I should run around the block
just to shove a thumb in the eyeball of nonbreath.
I should plaster jism all over the room. The mind
must be taught to cha-cha. If disorder were a hoodlum,
the imagination would be its zip gun. My brain flings
star bursts into the dark's dislocation. Who is this black-
booted abeyance who would make us squat down
on marble toilets with ours chins propped in cupped hands?
Better not yell, it sighs. Better eschew bad thoughts.
Even the critic—conduit or condom—doesn't he or she
seek to limit? Like a mother crying out, Don't run!
A nit-picking tut tut. So immobility has made another pal.
We are besieged by whisperers going Hush. What a balance
between too much breathing and not enough. Isn't entropy
the very devil—immobility's helpmate urging the Slowdowns
to rest? I prefer to think of those Nordic depredators
taking their enemies to a hilltop. Two cuts in the back
and they grab their victim's lungs. Then they yank.
The point is to see how far you run before you drop
with the wind making a high howling through the holes.
Let's call it metaphor. At least they gave their best.

■ ■ ■

Said the lady: I prefer the absurdity of writing poems
to the absurdity of not writing poems. But she said it
in Polish. Another fellow said, You can't expect art
to be more than useless, which is no reason to stop.
Just beyond my front door, the bougainvillea rears up
the very size and shape of a Tyrannosaurus Rex.

Though immobile, it sways and glitters in the breeze.
Come fall the bright blooms turn brown, drop off.
Then, wonder of wonders, in spring a few blossoms
redden at the top and we begin all over again.
No fruit, no smell, what good does it do? It makes
my heart flip-flop. One more smack in the face
of the immobile. You might think a dollar bill
would be another enemy of the inert. Not true.
Cash is its green-backed pal: a frog basking
on the lily pad of burgeoning immobility: bjork!
Dough's foe is motion; swag hates the cyclic shift.
But the flower, the poem, the sonata, the song:
all beauty is a form of eager activity. Within
its delicate body each daisy is a rowdy dance.
Though older than the rock on which she sits,
the Mona Lisa doo-wops and flips within her frame.
Can we partake of this? If beauty is a vehicle,
are we able to drive the car, and just how far?

■ ■ ■

Outside, the walls rise up a thousand feet.
Inside, the corridors zigzag down and down.
In a dungeon at the very bottom an old codger
clutches a fragment of brick, a scrap of stone,
the tip of a nail, and on the wall he has drawn
a landscape. Roses are in bloom. Trees beckon.
In the distance we see snow-capped mountains.
A path winds back from the bottom of the picture,
vanishing at the foot of the lavender foothills.
A dog sits by the path with a stick in its mouth,
its ears cocked to depict the concept of readiness.
The codger is in the process of sketching a figure:

an oldster not unlike himself, long beard and mane,
rags like the rags he is wearing. When he rises
we see it's himself he has drawn, a small fellow
with his arm outstretched, hand extended as if
from the wall and raising one finger. The codger
turns to the door to give us a wink. Then he pokes
out his own finger and the instant the two fingers
touch, the codger disappears. Surprise! Now look.
Do you observe how the man in the picture sets off
up the path and how the dog hurries to join him?

■ ■ ■

But that's not quite right. Think of another picture.
You are alone in the gallery. You scratch your ear.
You notice a picture of a man scratching his ear.
You stop scratching your ear, he stops as well.
You step toward him. He steps toward you. You lift
your hands above your head and do a silly dance.
He kicks up his feet and dances, too. It's simple:
I sing, I'm so sadly solo. He sings: O, solo mio.
But mostly he sings it prior and I stumble upon it.
Surely, the concept of homesickness existed before
Odysseus felt blue, but not for me. That dead Greek
smacked the nail on the head. Did I feel before art
showed me how I felt? I was no more than a squall.
I was a complaint stuck on top of a pair of legs.
We're not talking about lexicons of purple passion.
Say I like mustard on my orange sherbet. Is this
unique? In a book I find some jerk who likes it too.
So with loneliness, so with love. Thus I attach myself
to the chorus line of sunny sufferers: spangled tights,
high-heeled shoes, the Bleakettes are coming to a theater

near you. No longer is it one lonesome soldier lacking
an answer but a room full of I-Don't-Knows riling their lice:
your brothers and sisters in befuddlement. Isn't their
company preferable to having fun or chowing down
alone? Solitary nights, solitary days—no talking,
no laughing, no loving—to create only excrement
which only increases to the inanimate. No point
in piling dirt on top of your head before you drop.
Time for that when you enter the glossy hereafter.

■ ■ ■

In the penultimate version of our situation,
various prime movers group at the top of a stairs.
In the sugar-smeared fingers of each is gripped
a toy car containing a miniature startled figure.
The cars are pushed to the top step and given a poke.
Bump, bump. One may assume the members of the group
begin to shout and clap, but let's shift our focus
to the small startled figures. If one could speak,
he might inquire, What's the reason for this trip?
Ahead lies only furious descent while back behind
is vaguest memory. Perhaps he poses philosophic
questions, reflections as to metaphysical purpose,
distinctions between the ambulatory and immobile.
Perhaps he craves another road or form of travel.
Perhaps he leans back to enjoy the ride. Unluckily,
back on top the prime movers have begun to fight.
It is their nap time, or possibly they wish a snack:
marshmallow on crackers with melted chocolate.
And so they have come to neglect their toy cars.
Meanwhile the knuckles of the tiny figures turn white
as they grip steering wheels that are ornament only.

They rack their brains for reasons for their plight.
Hundreds of explanations spring to mind but none
exactly fits the context or takes into account his
or her indisputable importance. Perhaps descent
and brutal bouncing makes it hard to think straight.
At last one takes pad and pencil and begins to write.

■ ■ ■

Oh, immobility, how thoroughly you set yourself
against us. Gravity's buddy, entropy's pal.
Every stoplight becomes your flag. The erect
cop with his hand raised to articulate halt
wears your uniform, no matter the color; or rather,
he duplicates your gesture. The simple negative—
no, nein, nicht, nada, nyet—becomes a vote cast
in your favor. Silence is your national anthem,
a vulture your favorite bird, rust your flavor.
Meanwhile we trot: one foot forward, then the next.
Not straight, not crooked, but in a circle. Perhaps
we produce a few sparks. Perhaps we go toot toot.
My right hand extends to where it grips the shoulder
of the fellow straight ahead, perhaps my left grasps
the hand of the one jogging at my side. You get
the point. You might think that we are unhappy.
We are singing. True, it is nothing too lively,
but it is loud enough to let us shuffle our feet.
Immobility is the focus of our muted ruckus.
And the orchestra? Let's say a disembodied violin
hangs in the night air with its cracked bow jazzing
across the catgut. Scratch, scratch. You find it ugly?
It is the sum of earthly beauty. It plays the tune
that drives us forward. We have begun to love it,

just as we love the trudging feet, the beating heart,
the joys of flatulence, the rush of blood in the brain:
just a few of the roadsters on our daily racetrack.
I ponder this as I sit on my bed poking at my slippers.
Sunlight chips a morning wedge across the carpet.
Outside, the daily hammering is well advanced.
Time to get up, old carcass: to work, to work!
Set your feet among the flux! Drag your shadow
out across the land! It's time to mingle your shoes
with the buyers and sellers, one foot forward, then
the next. The reality? To bang your drum in the mortal
parade. And the dream? To believe yourself dancing.

PART THREE

HEART II

—————————■—————————

Old Moster never jokes; he only punishes.

M.C. Snopes—William Faulkner

NO TANGOS TONIGHT

Heart meets Death in a fashionable singles bar
and they dance. Why so standoffish? asks Death.
Why must you squeeze me so tight? asks Heart.
They take a few turns about the floor. You keep
trying to lead, says Death. You step on my feet,
says Heart. The room is smoky and the music loud.
Heart and his new partner spin round and round.
Why not come home with me tonight? asks Death.
Sorry, says Heart, being polite, I'm here with friends.
Heart tries to keep a space between them. Too bony,
he thinks, too cold. Death pats Heart on the bottom.
Won't you ditch your pals for me? Heart is stubborn.
I swore I'd only leave with them. Across the room,
the faces of his friends blur in the smoke. It's funny
how I get the last dance, says Death. But the night's
still young, says Heart. He takes a peek at his watch
but it's hidden within the folds of Death's dark cape.
The song goes on and on. The band fades from sight.
With every turn Death weighs more as Heart labors
to lug him across waxy floor. Won't someone cut in?
In my house, whispers Death, the lights are kept dim,
the rugs are thick. We could have a ball. The rhythm
swells to a calypso beat. Heart no longer feels his feet.
He hardly hears what Death is murmuring in his ear,
something about not having to drive a delivery truck.
And why does Death keep calling him Morgan? I beg
your pardon, says Heart, but Morgan's not my name.
The band falls silent; the vapors begin to disappear.

Death raises Heart's chin with a bony finger. I wish
you had told me that before. I see by my dance card
that our turn comes later. Maybe a tango or milonga.
Thanks at least for a taste of pleasures yet to come.
Heart is left by himself on the floor. Soon the faces
of his friends emerge through the smoke. Some laugh,
some are deep in thought. Heart returns to his seat.
One friend buys a round of drinks, another tells a joke
about a cat. Still in shock, Heart grasps that he nearly
threw them over for a stranger. He starts to remark:
How capricious are the bonds that link us to our fate.
But then a dance begins, a tango. Heart will sit it out.

THE MALDITOS MAKE
A RACKET

The banditos of memory gallop their sorry nags
around the yard of Heart's hacienda. They smack
their horses' butts with their dusty sombreros.
Caramba, they shout, and Yip, yip, yip. Heart
watches from the window with his head poked
over the sill. Yesterday his Federales had vowed
that these *chingadas* would torment him no longer.
They had been corralled, imprisoned, driven back
to the jungle. Now they show up wilder than ever.
The fat one with a greasy mustache who signifies
Heart's defeats—debts unpaid, projects unfinished.
The one-eyed one, his chest crossed with X-like
cartucheras who brings to mind Heart's lost loves.
The skinny one with a scar on his cheek depicting
for Heart the betrayed friends, the help not given,
the letters not written. Others can be imagined:
work bungled, deadlines unmet, simple ruination.
They gallop in front of Heart's windows, shooting
off their pistols. Such a nuisance. This was the day
Heart had set aside for meditation, when he meant
to critique his defects and turn over a new leaf.
No chance for that now. The *malditos* are making
too big a racket. Instead, he will sip some whiskey
and study his catalog of beautiful women. He will
limp forward making mistakes and accumulating
regrets, just like yesterday and the day before. Now

there is a hammering at the door. It's the fat one
with a printed invitation. Come ride with us, it asks.
They are eager for Heart to be their chief. They flatter
the brilliance of his failings and cheer his capacity
to be bad. Heart is touched. Maybe later, he mumbles.
The *banditos* crowd through the door. In no time,
the entire gang is lounging in Heart's living room,
sprawling on his bed, swiping snacks from the fridge.
How can he endure it? you ask. But don't you see
it's like this every day. Heart is their boss already.
The way they dress, the way they wave their guns,
it's all under his direction. And if they disappeared,
Heart would be crestfallen. He'd lose his credibility
as a vital sinner, an officer in the army of the bad,
and be like you or me or anyone—just a civilian.

TO EXIST IN THE
GIVEN MINUTE

A long stick with a hook and a first rate fly reel—
such is Heart's gadget to correct his hasty nature.
You see, he's forever going off half-cocked, leaping
with eyes glued shut, and the result, in Heart's book,
is bruises, mostly in the interior, because while Heart's
exterior is as smooth as a baby's, his insides duplicate
a knotted mass of scar tissue. Oh, Heart has been hurt.
He's suffered setbacks and rejection. And the reason?
Heart blames the premature ejaculation of his emotions.
So he invents a tool to calm himself down. The hook
snags his belt in back. The stick rests on his shoulder.
When Heart must slow himself up, he cranks the reel
which exerts restraint enough to permit him to rethink
the logic of whatever propels him forward. But such
is Heart's nature that he's forever winding in the reel,
which explains why his posture, once erect, now slants
to forty-five degrees as if Heart were permanent victim
of permanent windstorm or stood on a schooner's prow
in the midst of Typhoon Adolf. Does it work? you ask.
Not as Heart would like. His fishing pole gets in the way
on buses. Several times he's given passersby an unlucky
smack, which has led to unfortunate remarks. So Heart
is forever muttering, Sorry, sorry, and knuckling his brow.
In fact, the pole's effect is to distract Heart to the extent
that he can think of nothing but it, which affords a modicum
of check. Success! But these fixations with past and future:

resentment and regret occupying the antiquity of one's life,
while desire and anxiety point ahead—how they badger
the here and now, until every particle of time gets packed
in the pint-sized second, making the single jiffy impossibly fat,
yet providing no room for Heart. *Now* has no time for now,
which leads Heart to catapult forward or dwell in the past,
which is not a solution but only increases his confusion.
Heart wonders who claims for time a linearity when clearly
it's a spiral. Is the problem philosophical or psychological?
Perhaps a pill could set Heart to rights. But what he wants
is the chance to stick in the minute, to live his sixty seconds
without peering into the past or future. It's not a fishing reel
Heart needs but blinders so nothing interferes with putting
one foot after the other. How we exaggerate our condition,
as if we shared our plight with angels and not the lesser beasts.
First the blinders, then a bridle, then a harness, at last a saddle.
Heart's life is a cart he hauls up a road made muddy by perplexity.
And what's his complaint? That he has sufficient brain to grasp
the basic problem. Wouldn't a lobotomy solve this difficulty?
Then what would happen to his delight in the wave's repetition,
a ragged line of geese across an autumn sky, the sound of rain—
all the negligible stuff he neglects, overlooks, or forgets he likes?

LOGO OF FIXED
BEWILDERMENT

In Fragonard's painting of the girl on the swing,
the young lady's stockinged foot points to the edge
of the canvas before, in one's fancy, she falls back.
Mood swings, mood swings, thinks Heart, I got
them bad. Sometimes up, sometimes elsewhere.
Not simply a pendulum of emotion, but three
hundred and sixty degrees of radical possibility,
a modal gyroscope of sensibility as Heart is whirled
from melancholy to ecstasy to animosity in the time
it takes a sparrow to flop from a branch, but that
is only part of the story, because Heart's adrenaline
which determines his degree of activity may function
at cross purposes with his disposition, so he can be
gloomy while energetic or jolly while half asleep.
To help Heart sort this out he also has a horoscope,
so on a day when he feels great his chart may tell him
to stay in bed. In addition are Heart's boils, pimples,
warts, which may plague him or not, frequent colds,
allergies, perhaps the flu, as well as various externals;
e.g., he can only be cheerful if he wears his blue shirt,
but his blue shirt is in the wash. Heart feels fortunate
if he knows who he is from one moment to the next,
which brings up his memory which is like anybody's:
flawed. So if he recalls last Monday as happy or sad
he's often mistaken. As for last week, Heart has only
an indistinct idea, making past and future equally dim,

while subjectivity and shifting biases compose the filter
through which Heart sees the world, if he can be said
to see the world at all. Such is the mixture that is Heart,
and if he didn't have a file cabinet of paper from doctor,
plumber, butcher, and all the rest declaring who he was,
he would have to carry above his head, much as an angel
wears a halo, a question mark of silver, as if Heart's logo
of fixed bewilderment was only a halo bent out of shape.
Once he has this figured out such phrases as *To my mind*
or *In my opinion* depend upon the phase of moon, season
of the year, and what Heart ate for lunch, while an inquiry
like How's it going? can bring Heart to a halt, make him
check his pulse, take a peek in a pocket mirror and state,
I don't care to admit and just what do *you* think I look like?
Then, having posed the question, he'll await your definition,
hoping to take that day's interpretation of Heart from you.

THE WORLD'S
MASTER PLAN

Baby bird with uplifted beak. Kitten, calf, or pup
with lips affixed to mother's teat—Heart ponders
the nature of manna. How the notion of its descent
from Heaven must have begun at mother's breast.
Heart loves to eat, to shove the world in his mouth,
to digest it lickety-split so he can start all over again.
Is this a throwback to the time when Heart pressed
his lips to his mother's nipple? Heart's recollection
is inexact. But in a Bible he finds a sketch of antique
Hebrew folk dashing helter-skelter about the desert
in flowing robes with their mouths tilted upward,
catching leaflets of foodstuffs pelting from the sky—
is this why some clouds are, vaguely, tit-shaped?
The point for Heart is that the concept of eating
begins with falling. Would his pleasure be greater
if he launched his daily bread with a food catapult,
then plucked it from the air with sturdy mandibles?
This for Heart would have anecdotal interest only.
Instead, he'd like to examine how the act of eating
fits in with the world's master plan, how the food's
descent and upward slant of the expectant mouth
enacts our existential melodrama, as if this everyday
activity formed an emblem of our mortal journey.
Heart's notion is that Nature's strategy is to hasten
a variety of nutriment through a creature's system
in a manner somewhat the opposite of distillation,

since what is made is dirt, and thus the earth swells
ever fatter—night soil, topsoil, organic compounds.
So what does it matter what Heart pitchforks down
his throat as long as he continues to excrete and add
his tuppence to the planet's perpetual expansion?
Doughnuts forever, thinks Heart. How right to take
a bite from whatever can fit his mouth, which means
cannibalism is only wrong because it robs the world
of one more digestive system. Heart has always known
that feeding was a form of love, taking from and passing on,
the gourmand as fervent middleman, who by constant
defecation constructs the globe on which he stands.

TO BLOW YOUR ENEMY A FINAL KISS

Heart's two feet are stuck two feet deep in the muck.
It's spring and he is happy, sort of. Chestnut leaves
burst forth. Daffodils sprout lunatic with yellow.
Each creature on the farm, whether bird or goat,
broods on sex: some sing, some smack their heads
against rocks. So though Heart is stuck he has plenty
to look at and he feels content, sort of. After all
he has enough to eat, the weather is warm, the sky
is free from any hint of rain. Isn't this what Heart
has always sought, a location of his own? So what
if he can't move his feet? His eyes roam as they will.
Physically he could be a Grecian pillar, but mentally
he's as free as Marco Polo. And Heart is not alone.
Other workers on the farm are stuck as well. None
seems unhappy, while some would say their planting
is of their choosing and, should they wish, they could
easily depart. Not Heart. He knows his feet are stuck,
though of course he will tell you he's content, sort of.
The animals admire him, sort of. His colleagues are not
close enough to interfere with his daydreams or what
Heart calls his process of thought. The food is almost
what anyone might want and Heart could readily spend
his life and not move a foot as the beasts are raised
and reaped with Heart stock-still in one plot of dirt.
But often at night when breezes waft across his brow,
Heart wonders why he's not happier. When he checks

his needs, he finds them all fulfilled. He lacks for naught.
So what if he can't agitate his feet. A runner, he isn't.
Explorer, bunion grower, toe-hound, shoe fetishist—
such activities leave him apathetic. Even when mobile
Heart inclined toward the sedentary: inspiring thoughts,
dreams supreme, a little note taking—such is Heart's work.
So, although he hates being stuck in the muck, his logic
shows this a salutary spot and even his complaint about
lack of movement must be wrong. Heart nods his head
in reluctant agreement and endures one more dreary day
before he starts making kissing faces at the goat. He twists
his lips, sticks out his ruby tongue, and goes smack, smack.
The goat is appalled and turns away, such is the moral depth
of a brute who if allowed would subsist entirely on tin cans.
Was this the reason it came to the farm? Of course Heart
can assert that he is preparing the goat for any extremity,
since what lies ahead for the goat is slaughter, that it exists
not to think and browse and admire the sunset but to fix
for some happy group—wedding party or wake—a banquet
of goat chop, goat loin, goat flank. But to refer to the future
is apart from Heart's job description. He is here to decorate
the goat's present labor, not to speak of what comes next.
Heart rolls back his lips and puffs his cheeks, as if he were
an amatory buffoon who longed to squash his cranial labia
against the brute's inglorious mustache. Aghast, the goat
can recall nothing to approach Heart's unjustified assault
on its goatish self-regard and pride; and soon its cerebellum
turns to retribution. Trotting back a dozen yards, the goat
drops its head and hurdles forward, a miniature locomotive
with horns lowered. When struck, Heart is knocked snout
over rump, landing on his butt in a manure heap. Finding

his feet unfettered Heart thinks: I'm free! He blows the goat
a parting kiss and trots toward the ivy-covered pillars which
mark the farm's outer gate. Here he looks back: Should he
return to litigate against the goat? Heart won't push his luck.

For E. B. V.

CORN TO POUND
TO MAKE HIS BREAD

Snakeroot, bloodroot, smartweed, nipplewort—
Heart has pitched his tent in a bosky dell far
from the honking horns and automotive abuse
of diurnal intercourse. Although he'll miss
his friends, he is tired of the ups and downs
of human emotion. If such must be his lot,
then he'll pledge his heart to Otis the Elevator
and seek out sexual relief between floors. Better
to retreat to the dusky woods and build his hut
in the robin-crowded glade. There he'll explore
the words of the early saints and at times jot down
a poem, though for his eyes only. You know how
in any sporting event even the game's top player
must take a breather upon the bench? Likewise Heart.
In his long life, how many Valentines has he sent?
How many windows has he belted his heart out
underneath? If love stirs the air, then Heart's name
should be fixed to an up-coming hurricane. But that
was before. Now he hopes to rest. He has a flute
he'll learn to play. He'll do sketches of monkshood
and dutchman's britches, plant a dozen rows of life-
sustaining crops. Not meat, Heart believes, it might
be meat that caused the trouble. A few nuts. Corn
to pound to make his bread. Heart needs only this.
Waking early, he watches the sun crest the viburnum.
Dew glitters on spreading dogbane. One butterfly

flits in quest of another. Birds sing courtship songs.
Heart feels a prickling in his crotch which he ignores.
He refuses to be bullied by the reproductive cycle.
His thoughts will be his offspring. Soon he'll produce
a small book of aphorisms, advice poetically expressed
on how to live, love, and think. Heart exults on the start
of a new life. Never has he seen a spot so fertile. One
honeybee chases another beneath the hairy bush-clover.
Blossoms unveil the entire range of fragrance and color;
a rabbit gallops after its mate; one deer butts another—
while Heart squats in solitary pursuit of straying penseés.
Wordless balloons cruise his brain in monotonous strings.
His pen rests idea-less upon the page. The day drags by
as nature's creatures search out amorous adventures.
This is Hell, Heart says at last. By noon he's packed his tent.
Back in town, he stops at the first strip joint he can find.
Take it off! He shouts to a girl with Styrofoam extensions.
Heart is eager to regulate his breathing, revitalize his pulse.
He fears that country-life might have damaged his virility.
That night Heart takes a lady to a bistro for slabs of meat.
Over drinks he says, Solitude was meant for the immobile
and inorganic, for stones and dirt, but all animate things
require a full range of intercourse—social, mental, sexual—
which makes men strong. Then, as he caresses her foot
with his dusty brogan, he adds: And ladies too, of course.

SCATTERED OAKS
IN FULL LEAF

Why must calm and reasonable behavior make up
one's emotional exoskeleton, wouldn't it be better
to rage and run about and let a serene and sensible
disposition be the dominion of one's interior? Such
is Heart's belief. To illustrate he points to the people
who ride the bus he takes to work, reading newspapers
or looking from the window in apparent tranquillity
while bitten nails and bent backs suggest an internal
landscape where primitive creatures gnash and feed
amid steaming vents, and the whole business tucked
in the victim's belly or cerebral equivalent. No wonder
most smiles on the street mimic a wince, that the spine
beneath the tailored suit duplicates a corkscrew shape.
How many people conceal a crime they think unique,
fantasies they imagine divide them from the human family,
the belief that their hands alone are stained by squalor?
Thus each feels he or she hides a secret, as if the facade
of good manners and sensible behavior formed a jail cell
in which a brute paced back and forth, a monster never
beheld on the planet. Is this why they walk so cautiously,
speak so precisely as if they feared the cage might break
and set loose this storied beast and they would be exiled
everlastingly? And so they strive to appear calm and keep
their faces vacant just to make certain their secret remains
unguessed. Wouldn't it be better if the business were reversed?
Let's say the offense was obvious to all. Go ahead,

kick a nun in the butt, put a cork up a cop's snout. Heart
is willing to bet that once the crime was brought to light,
its size would shrink till tyrannosaurus turned to tortoise
and what stayed unique was that it stayed hidden for so long.
But even if someone decided to be bad, consider the calm
of the interior: green meadows stretching to the horizon,
scattered oaks in full leaf, a place to linger when the outside
got wild, a necessary retreat; or this is how it seems to Heart
whose interior is like a sea teeming with malignant creatures
while the outside, at best, assumes a blue unruffled surface.
Good day, good day, he calls to one and all. The assertion
itself erecting the exoskeleton which fastens him together,
a framework without which he'd constrict to a violent jelly,
a cage protecting Heart's shy panther from public exposure.
Oh, how he'd prefer to permit his exterior to rage as it might
while he crept away to the exact tranquillity of his inner part:
morning light bedecking the palm trees, blue vaults ascending.

THE LIGHT IS DUSKY, THE SHADOWS LONG

When people speak of recurring dreams, Heart gets quiet.
Instead of telling what he knows, he changes the subject.
As you might suspect, he has his own repeating dream
to disturb his nights and upset his days in which he rides
a tricycle down a cobblestone street, while not far away,
but always getting closer, rumbles a steamroller. Heart
peddles down one alley after another as the cobblestones
jitter his brittle bones and skew his trike from left to right.
The streets are narrow and if he and the steamroller met,
Heart would be crushed flat. Always the light is dusky,
the shadows long. Some people have exciting dreams
that repeat each night: tales of money, sex, heroic deeds.
Not Heart. Till dawn breaks he rides his trike. Why can't
he just climb off? you ask. Surely he'd be faster on foot.
But in his dream Heart seems shackled to his machine.
One might say that he has trikelike aspects in his soul,
and so Heart and trike, like a centaur, make up one unit.
And why fall silent when the subject of dreams is broached?
Wouldn't Heart prefer to admit his plight? But recently
it seems that he has heard this steamroller while awake.
He'll be up late standing on a bridge, watching the river
roil and tumble far beneath, when, off in the distance
he'll hear a rumbling. Or he'll wake near dawn and ask
what just woke him. Lifting his head, he listens, holding
his breath, and at times he hears the grinding of metal
against stone, the booming of the cylinder, a tuneless

note far below what anyone could sing, a note that finds
its way up from underground. And so Heart considers
resettling in another city and avoids the subject of dreams.
And he plays harder or more noisily, singing and laughing
with friends, although he seems to take no pleasure in it,
and sometimes he walks to the door and listens, or stops
on a foggy street and tilts his head, then steps along faster.
Heart asks how many others have this clamor in their lives,
a tumult starting in dream and soon taking up every hour.
Is this why they seem confused? Do they fear to be thought
the only ones and worry that folks will think them crazy?
So they fall silent when they hear that noise in the distance,
for some a scraping, for others a moan. And the lucky ones,
who say they hear nothing, maybe they haven't learned to listen—
as when someone, meaning to do a favor, draws your attention
to a birdcall that you have never noticed or haven't bothered
to distinguish from the miscellany of daily noises, but now,
once its special note has been pointed out, you hear all round.

LET'S PEEK AT THE
DENTAL WORK

Whoops, Heart loses a tooth, then another.
His friends hold a raffle. How many teeth
will be left when death drops the final curtain?
Fifteen or twenty? Heart asks if the money
will go to charity? Sure, says his pal Woody.
The charity of the self. His friends yuk it up.
Each invests a hundred bucks. It's a bull market.
Their assets swell. Then Heart loses a molar.
His pal Woody is downcast. I guess I'm knocked
out of the shooting match. I needed the dough.
Heart says, Maybe I can lend you a little cash.
Woody's as happy as a lark. That would be great.
A few months later, Heart loses another tooth.
Another friend gets blue. For you it's a tooth,
he says, for me it's a retirement cottage. So Heart
offers him a loan as well. Will he get it back?
Heart suspects not. His pals rub their hands.
They ask: How's the old mouth? In the midst
of their attention, Heart feels strangely lonely.
How would his chums respond to naked gums?
Though Heart and his pals have various needs,
Heart's aging choppers become the focal point
of the relationship, not good deeds, nor slaps
on the back. No longer do his pals meet his eye,
they eye his lips. They wait for Heart to open
his mouth, but it's not kind words they seek,

but to peek at the dental work. For days, Heart
stays home and broods about what to do next.
Then he visits a slaughterhouse and buys a bag
of bull's teeth. Each is the size of Heart's fist.
He sends a tooth to every friend with the note:
Sorry to put a crimp in your future but you lose.
Heart's examination of self-perception has led
to the conclusion that if one's view on flat land
is fifteen miles, then one's interior perspective
is less than a block; not that his friends meant
to be mean or are short of brain but Heart felt
their somnolent conscience needed a metaphoric
kick in the butt, a reminder to value handshakes
and pats over stocks, bonds, and bucks. Presto!
The pals liquidate their assets and throw a party.
For two weeks in a cottage on the beach they feast,
frolic, and fornicate. Heart makes a friendly visit.
One night he stands on the shore as the waves roll in.
A full moon lights the sky. He thinks of the extra-
terrestrials who have built their cities on the moon's
back part. Doesn't intimacy also have its dark side?
During these happy days, Heart keeps his mouth shut,
drinks with a straw, hides his teeth lest trouble starts.

BETWEEN THEM ROSE
THE BONER OF CONTENTION

Heart checks into a revitalization clinic
for a crick in his back but files get mixed up
and when he climbs from the therapeutic tub,
his penis has swollen to gigantic proportions.
It looks like a zeppelin or robust cigar. Sorry,
says the doc, mistakes happen. It will shrink back
in a few days. To get to his car Heart puts a box
over his member and pretends to carry a package.
It's so imposing that Heart expects it to recite Yeats.
Once home he refuses to leave the house. Pals visit.
Two take snapshots. Others yuk it up. At times
like this friends are no help. If Heart broke his leg,
he'd get lots of sympathy, but no one cares squat
about a big prick. Two days later he has to go out.
He puts a bag over his penis but it's too awkward
so he decides to use paint, and when it's complete,
his vital part looks like a bunch of green bananas
which Heart is toting down the street. Folks stare
but not as they might if they knew the true nature
of his affliction. As for Heart, he feels distracted,
otherwise he might spot the newspaper headline: Zoo
Wagon in Pileup—Monkeys Escape. After a block
Heart hears a chattering in the trees above him.
Before he can glance up an ape leaps on his prick
and tries to take a bite. Heart knocks the brute off
and starts to run. The monkeys follow lickety-split.

It's hard to be quick while packing a stack of bananas
between your legs, but Heart does his best, dashing
through restaurants, back alleys, along the hallways
of municipal buildings. The apes are fleet of foot,
but the fright they incite in Heart's heart makes him zip.
Soon he gets trapped in a cul de sac. What lousy luck.
With his back to a brick wall, Heart watches the brutes
trot toward him chattering and making monkey grins.
Between them rises the boner of contention, its paint
flecking off but still looking bananalike. Heart lifts
a hand in order to speak; the monkeys pause to listen.
Here, says Heart, is a parable on the nature of ambition,
how what is wished for overwhelms, till the wish itself
wrecks the object of desire. The monkeys nod but none
takes notes. Again they approach. A few carry forks,
others wrap napkins around their necks. Now at last
the clinic's potion wears off. With a whistling, Heart's
member deflates. The apes look stricken. All that's left
of his tumescence is a green pinkie, an emerald smidgen.
The monkeys scratch their noggins. Heart zips his pants.
It starts to rain. But for Heart it feels as if the weather
had turned sweet. Saluting the departing apes, he thinks:
Ambition, it leads to naught. Surely, it would be better
to go back to the days of basic pleasures—kindergarten,
for example, a prepubescent location, that time before
he ever knew what deceptions adulthood held in store,
when holding hands held no purpose past holding hands
and life's biggest riddle was whether his two o'clock snack
would be milk or lemonade, Fig Newtons or ginger snaps.

GOD'S POORER PARTICLE, I.E., THE DEVIL

After Heart's pal Frank gets mushed in a car wreck,
Heart hurls rocks at the sky just to show God what
he thinks of such conduct—not that Heart necessarily
has faith but he wants to take this chance to indicate
his thoughts on the entire set up: folks brought forth
onto this earth, knocked about for a typical stretch,
then dragged out in ways that cheapen what scant
dignity they've struggled hard to build up. So Heart
finds a rock, water polished and perfect for his palm.
The day, apart from Heart's loss, is a radiant example
of what is possible in early spring, but for Heart, without
his pal, it's incomplete so he flings his rock skyward,
then goes off to get another. As a result, when the rock
plummets back and smacks Heart on his schizocarp,
he's shocked and wonders if he should take it as a sign,
for while Heart is no believer he'd like to cultivate belief.
If a fellow flung a rock at Heart, wouldn't he fling it back?
This becomes Heart's proof that God exists. Who else
would hurl a rock at Heart but the one Heart wished to hit?
And if God, being good, wouldn't lob a rock, then the lump
suggests that the culprit must be God's poorer particle, i.e.,
the Devil. Thus, Heart's evidence of God is the conduct
of his opposite—No Devil, no God is how Heart sees it—
and Heart's got the bump to prove it. At the funeral home,
where Frank is on display, Heart finds additional proof,
since his pal in death looks better than alive—they've even

fixed his busted nose. Why else make Frank pretty except
to attend eternity's party, whether in Heaven with a harp
or toasting on a rotisserie down below? Frank looks great,
which convinces Heart there might be life after life after all.
But you know how sometimes someone spots the Virgin
or random saint in his garden and millions crush the daisies
to grab a bit of blessed dirt? After Heart declares his proof,
he hawks snapshots of his lump and briefly acquits himself
of spiraling credit card debt, at least until the bulge deflates
giving him a skull like any others, which is why he can soon
be seen dashing about his yard heaving rocks Heavenward
to snag a new lump, while the Devil, it seems, flings them back
but misses, until Heart falls flat. Has our hero croaked? Nope.
Instead, he asks if these rocks cast wide of the mark are meant
to mock or are misses only. So the fact that he stays unstruck
must signify a sort of proof, but, of what, Heart asks, of what?

THAT STUFF ABOUT
A BETTER PLACE

It seems to Heart that people are dying at a faster rate
than usual. Whichever way he turns another old friend
is kicking the bucket, and the acquaintances and friends
of friends—rushing pell-mell toward death's dark cleft,
the tunnel-mouth leading to a twilight-land, as if Death
were offering an autumnal sale on elemental departure
so it's best to buy now. Each person to whom Heart talks
has a tale—a bank president zapped in his sleep, a baker
tripped up by cancer's wolf pack, a poet nixed by a stroke.
Alone in their lives, in their exit they form such a throng
that Heart spends each day in a state of flinch. No longer
does he say, Hello; he asks, Who's living? And whenever
he visits the dying, he sees that none believes that bunkum
about entering a better place, the holiday spot of no return.
Each friend who disappears constructs a chasm in the air,
making a Dalmatian-colored sky, a sievelike atmosphere.
Heart visits sickbeds to give support. He tells his chums
how much he needs them. He offers bribes to stay alive.
A dying pal shrugs. Given the choice, he'd go to the beach.
Perhaps, thinks Heart, the problem lies with the morticians
or gravediggers, maybe like much else the cause is economic—
packed cemeteries, too few tombstones, not enough coffins
to go around—the tricks of capitalists who squeeze a profit
from sticking Heart's pals in the dirt so quick. Wouldn't it
be better to let the dead hang around for a week to see if any
might perk up? Surely some were only fooling. No doubt

one or two would stroll back and pick up the yoke. Heart wants to know: What did we do wrong that Death should despise our lives? Spiritual pimples? Insolent soul stench? Often it seems that Heart cannot say farewell fast enough. Whichever way he turns, someone is dying behind his back. Even the young, even the happy. It's as if the still animate were falling from clouds or were like baby birds toppling from ill-built nests. The deficient featherless creatures don't have the sense to stay put. As a result, Heart scurries about trying to snag and grab them from the air, seeing tumbling shadows from the corner of his eye, scrambling this way and that, making diving misses as his friends go splat, splat.

THE SORRY FRONDS
OF THE PALM TREES

Dressed in white and driving a white panel truck
with the words Pest Control painted on the doors,
Heart pursues the worm of gloom, the termite
of misery, the flea of despair. In his notebook
he carries blown-up snapshots taken through
a microscope that show their hypodermic smiles,
the minuscule prickers that make you itch. Heart
loves his work. Now that he has discovered
that the forces of sadness are an alien manifestation,
he can begin at once to hunt them out. He recalls
the old days when he sprawled in bed unable to rise
because melancholy, seemingly, danced on his chest.
Now he knows that melancholy is a tiny creature
with an ugly kisser gnawing on his nether parts.
If the natural state of humankind is joy, he thinks,
then it follows that all the negatives are external.
Heart stops his truck at the first house on his list.
A gloomy oldster in a gray sweater opens the door.
No money 'til later, says the codger, a disbeliever.
But Heart briskly gets busy, spraying and swatting.
Before he's half done, the old guy is on the phone
inviting over some girls. Soon ragtime cranks up
on the stereo as Heart digs out insects from every
cranny and nook. An hour later the job is complete,
but Heart can scarcely escape before high-strutters
in bikini tops and leather miniskirts mount the steps.

Hipsters disembark from a block-long private bus.
Back in his truck, Heart checks his book. A full day
of bug bashing lies ahead, but strangely Heart feels
a little low. Then he spots a red splotch on his wrist
where one of the codger's pests has pricked him.
Heart drives to a cliff above the beach and parks.
Cold rain whips the sorry fronds of the palm trees.
In the dark clouds he sees his last moments approach.
In the gray water he sees the futility of his endeavor.
Heart blows his nose and wonders what it's all about
as he patiently waits for the poison to exit his system.

HIS FAVORITE BLUE CUP

Over the years—and Heart has had many years—
numerous objects have slipped from his possession,
some were lost, some fell apart, some got stolen.
That cowboy doll he loved as a child,
does a piece of it still remain? And the pen
he's been looking for all week, where does it hide?
His favorite blue cup which the dog broke,
the green linen shirt that at last wore out,
the Chevie convertible that wound up in the junkyard—
Heart has come to think that all these objects are together
along with absent friends, departed family members,
and pets that traveled over to the great beyond.
Somewhere, he believes, there's a place made up
of previous houses, former gardens, and furnished
with the vanished furniture his hands have touched.
There missing friends recline on once-loved chairs.
A cat gone for twenty years naps beneath a burning lamp.
Lost clothes fill the closets, lost books line the shelves.
The trees in front, cars in back: Heart would know them all.
These days Heart's mind sometimes wanders.
He's in a daze, he's drifted off or gathering wool,
and he thinks at such times he, too, has disappeared,
that he's rambling through his composite house,
sipping coffee from his blue cup, tossing a ball
for a mutt he owned when he was six, or walking
arm and arm with a friend not seen for a dozen years.
You look pale, the friend says, you've gotten thinner.
I've been away, says Heart, I've been away.

WHY IS HE SUDDENLY PARALYZED?

Sometimes the sky is so blue that it makes Heart sad,
as if beauty intensified transformed joy to heartache.
Heart can't understand it. For instance, this morning
as sunlight glistened on the new snow and white birch,
and not one cloud dared show its face. The chickadees
above the bird feeder flitted in figure-eights and Heart's
chest cavity felt ready to burst. Then wonder turned
to sadness and he asked, What's taking place inside me?
Why do I feel suddenly paralyzed? Shouldn't splendor
make me sing and leap about? Within his breast, Heart
felt an expansion that rapidly increased until an explosion
seemed imminent and he got ready to shout, Watch out!
Then all turned dim. Not dark, but pensive and existential,
as if he were a fixed spot in the midst of gyrating rapidity.
Heart has run against this feeling before: in the museum,
for instance, seeing a favorite painting—Bellini Madonna
or Cézanne landscape—a near blowout in the blood pump
that turned to gloom. Is this a mental version of the swift
descent from lofty peaks that sometimes follows orgasm?
Or what he felt in his youth when the bars closed at night:
empty streets, padlocked doors, and a head full of party?
But this emotion when faced with beauty holds no regret,
or of anything being over, unless its melancholy pressure
is in fact the pressure in the chest preceding a heart attack.
But why does it hit him so strongly on a bright winter morning?
Heart's not complaining. He wants to figure it out. Maybe

it's a sense of his own irrelevance next to beauty's immensity, although Heart has no wish to be made bigger. Or possibly it's the perception of ephemeral duration, Heart's back flip through life, next to beauty's perpetuity, even though Heart has no wish to live longer than usual. Whatever the answer, Heart believes it's a sense of scale with him stuck on the side of the small. Does this disturb his ego? Heart presumes not. This morning life planted a smooch on his delicate passage and flitted away. Stunned, Heart hurried off to find someone to tell. The first person he met was the mailman on his rounds. I just received the most incredible gift, said Heart, knowing that he wasn't getting it right. Already the moment was fading. The mailman gave a wave and crossed the street. The burden of his work affords no room for chitchat and he has grown accustomed to the importunities of dreamers such as Heart.

IT'S NOT THE HOOKERS
OR OPIUM DENS

Heart decides that when you die your wrinkles
go back to the shop. His best friend Woody
kicked the bucket but before he went under
all his wrinkles slipped from his skull, leaving it
as smooth as a toddler's. Of course, it's different
with car accidents and murder, violent departures
without the chance for neutralizing cogitation,
but old folks slipping away—it's like turning in
old light bulbs or taking bottles back for deposit.
Sweatlike, the corrugations slide from the skull.
So Heart thinks there must be a spot where worn
out wrinkles are kept. It's not in the phone book,
nor classified ads, but deep in a neglected alley
must lie a warehouse where great bins are filled
with chin wrinkles, forehead, and cheek wrinkles,
all tagged and labeled. Heart wants to pay a visit.
His own deepening furrows he finds unenthralling,
but if he could wear Woody's or another friend's,
then each time he looked in the mirror he would be
calling them back just a little. Instead of detecting
burgeoning decrepitation, he would be claiming
connection, even saying hello to an old companion.
So that is why Heart can be found at times down
in the warehouse district so late at night. It's not
the hookers or opium dens or even illegal roulette
that attract him; rather he feels certain that in one

of those ramshackle structures the defunct wrinkles
of the newly dead are kept and when Heart finds it,
why, it will be like decking himself out with ribbons,
except when he looks in the mirror he will see a bit
of Greasy or Woody or Frank: a pal map of dead faces,
their half-forgotten physiognomies physically reborn,
unearthed ex-chums, the dear departed together again.

THE ERSATZ METAPHYSIC
OF COMMERCIALISM

Heart wonders why he's such a sucker
for the Cadillacs of life, the Porsches
of pleasure. In place of Grape Nuts,
he prefers lobster. Instead of polyester,
he favors the touch of silk. Buy faster,
throw away faster, becomes his motto.
Shouldn't he be content with cotton?
But Heart has no trace of the ascetic.
He only eats to eat again, a turbo-driven
revolving door for the world's goods,
a cliff face for a Niagara of accumulation.
Should I cut back? he asks. Yet TV, radio,
newspaper ads, the tips of consumerism's
many icebergs, menace the canoe of his life
and from each comes a singing, vowing
to love Heart alone—Captain Odysseus
of the S. S. *Titanic*—till the pursuit of buying
takes priority over what is bought. But wait.
Is this Heart's style? Isn't he victim of a malady
of soul? Heart is certain that given the option,
he'd wear only white, feast on bean sprouts,
then for dessert a single grape. What's the source
of his acquisition fixation? To find out he follows
the hawkers of the ersatz metaphysic of commercialism,
until one leads him through a hole in the ground.
Is it Satan or the ghost of J. P. Morgan? But Heart

is out of date. Entropy is the Prime Mover of our century.
Muscular stokers shovel coal into its furnaces—
gigantic steam pipes and pistons—no wonder
Entropy wants us to buy big: the faster spent,
the sooner gone. Above the bustle, the Prime Mover
oversees its crew from a glass-enclosed office.
Take a look at those sketches tacked to the wall—
you've seen how architects surround themselves
with plans to show how the future will be? Ditto
Entropy. No earth, sky, or sea: a true democracy
of temperature and matter. Entropy rubs together
its dainty paws: a world resolved into the chaos
from which it sprang but with the ruckus gone,
not a single vibration, all colors ashen, no horizon.

DOG-TIRED CANNON FODDER WON'T SALUTE

At times Romance has wrinkles which even Heart
is unable to surmount and by which he feels defeated
as when his prick refuses to jump to its feet and sing,
and Heart asks if he should resort to Popsicle sticks
or beetle-driven crane to make it stand erect. At times
Old Pud won't leave its self-hole. Heart lies on his back
and plays the flute. Snake won't dance. Heart shows it
snapshots of naked ladies in the military dress of love,
but dog-tired cannon fodder won't salute. What's wrong?
Cat got your tongue? You'd rather read a dirty book? Old
number one's got the sulks. It wants their roles reversed,
to make Heart shrivel up, get zipped in his own pants.
So Pud squats down, refuses to quit his stall while Heart
is forced to explain—Of course I love you—to the lady
by his side. And it's true. Just the mention of her name
causes Pud to thrash about and groan. But it leads Heart
to wonder who's in charge, to ask who's boss. At times
Heart attempts to order his parts from big toe to ear tip,
those portions which, allegedly, he has under his control,
but more and more often his bones creak and joints balk.
Just what is Heart's affinity to this miscellany of the body?
Isn't he like a bungling shop steward, who, as he ages,
is increasingly disliked by his demanding constituency?
So he tries to win them back with ever bigger bribes: mood
stabilizers and vitamins pack his gut, eyes get new glasses,
while the flesh requires pricier items of fancy dress.

But then when Heart needs Pud most, Pud checks out.
He wants to sleep. Perhaps he writes a poem. Perhaps
he dreams. Why does it seem to Heart that he is losing
mastery over his own anatomy. Where is his authority?
                Gone.
Does each individual become his own defeated general,
which makes the path toward death the ultimate retreat
after the troops have fled? Heartbeat being the last soldier
to slip over the hill? But now in bed Heart must explain
to his current treasure the mounting dislike of his own
rebellious parts for their communal farm. Or, conversely,
isn't Pud a rat to skulk away from his bad luck ship?
Don't fret, says his ladylove, you're under lots of stress.
What's stress, thinks Heart, but bondage to the illusion
of control? In the beginning, his motor skills led a life
of their own as he thrashed about his crib, but bit by bit
Heart brought them under the yoke, even learning language
as a way to keep the world in check. Not that it worked
or not much. Was there ever a time when he felt that control
was what he had? For years it seemed to lie ahead, then,
inexplicably, one day it lay behind. Could Heart pinpoint
the exact spot? Guess not. Now Heart's component parts
totter away to their prior chaotic state, with each bodily
scrap trying to rule the roost, or seeking its personal bent.
Late that night Heart walks back to his car. On the sidewalk
under the streetlight's shining finger sparkles a silver dollar.
Heart feels a stirring in his pants. Is the sleepyhead awake?
Before Heart knows what's up, Old Pud, like a frog after a fly,
flips from his crotch and plucks the coin from the concrete.
And why, asks Heart, couldn't you have done that before?

UNTIL WE DROOL
AND PISS OURSELVES

Car honk, donkey bray, seal bark—it's only since
Heart has sat with dying friends, elderly and failing,
in hospital or home, that he has at last understood
what this discord in his daily life has taught him—
upshot ruckus, hubbub of the interior, shout for help
or invitation? Where does this racket come from?
Lungs, throat, the entire brute: not quite a cry, but
repeated nonetheless. With one pal, Heart counts
the clamor on his watch, thirty shouts per minute,
hour after hour, the truncated bay of the departing soul.
Heart had thought the noise unique but with friend
after friend he has heard it again—the protocadaver
trying to snatch sufficient breath for the failing motor.
Could it resemble a knock, the soul smacking its head
against Death's closed door? Could it resemble a shout
called out to the other world: Come quick, we're ready
to depart. Or is it a version of abbreviation? At times
Heart cries out in his sleep and the lady sharing his bed,
should Heart be so lucky, will critique his exclamation
as half-bark, half-bellow, which in dream was meant
as supplication, an eager appeal with reasons given,
nearly a philosophy of desperation, translated through
the wall of sleep into a single yap, like all the world's
books on a microchip or the relation between a strip
of beef jerky to a mature elk. Maybe his dying pals
did the same: a petition shrunk to a roar clipped short.

But does it ask for help or beg to depart? Is it perhaps
a reduction of hours of talk, the messages, last words,
the advice to a friend left unsaid—death bark, soul knock—
thirty per minute, two thousand per hour, all day long
and into the next and perhaps another after that, until
it slows, until it stops. Heart asks how anyone can stand
the horror. Not just friends and family, but the entire
medical profession, why don't they drop to their knees,
until the world has its hair turned white and we drool
and piss ourselves and pack our fists into our ears so deep
that the knuckles click together in the center of the skull.
It is then Heart begins to fathom the nature of education,
how an event that seems to exist by itself may prepare us
for inevitable nastiness: car honk, donkey bray, seal bark.
So Heart can say, I have heard this sound before, which
lets the buffeting become bearable. So instead of Heart's
thatch being turned to snow, it only gets a tad more gray;
instead of flinging himself down on the floor, his bones
only warp and shrink a trifle more. Walking along the street,
it strikes Heart once again: pedestrian shout, engine roar—
clamor priming us for the last hour, which lets us offer relief,
compassion, even to endure the death of another. But the rest
of the world's racket—shattering glass, garbage can clatter—
what does this prepare us for? How will it make the future
a spot we care to meet, what horror does it lessen by example?
So much of dissolution and decay lie ahead for Heart's attention,
for him to reflect upon as he makes his preparation. Possibly
this tumult, undefined, forms the footpath to that final death
beyond which no other will remain for him to mourn: his own.

HUNTING DOGS PURSUE THE WOUNDED DEER

Heart descends to Hell to look for old friends.
A mine-shaft connects to a ladder leading down.
Heart expects Hell to be smoky. Instead, it's damp.
The dead amuse themselves with video games.
A red-suited fellow passes out coins for free.
Hush, says Heart's pal, I'm winning. A race car
on a gigantic screen rushes along perilous roads.
During life this guy drove clunkers eaten by rust.
Now he's hit the big time. Heart wanders off.
Another friend tells Heart: This won't take long.
On the screen a man dashes through a supermarket.
He has sixty seconds to load his cart for nothing.
In life, his pal pinched pennies till they squealed.
Now his minute lasts forever. A third friend says,
I got the highest score, give me a moment more.
His screen is packed with nude ladies whom he tries
to pitch through hoops. During life he was so shy
even talking to the cat took brass. Now he's boss.
Heart walks about until his friends are ready to chat.
Among the famous dead he sees Eurydice chained
to a pinball machine, Achilles deep in war games.
Everyone works very hard. Why is Hell so damp?
It comes from soggy underarms and sweaty brows.
Heart goes back to the friend driving the race car.
Getting settled in? asks his chum. Just a jiffy more,
then we'll have a long talk. Heart touches his arm:

Are you happy? A fretful look clouds his pal's brow,
then it fades as he zigzags toward a hairpin turn.
The furrow of distress in his perception has passed.
Heart seeks out the exit. At the door a demon tells him—
We're devising *your* personalized diversion even now,
a parable concerning hunting dogs and a wounded deer.
Back on earth, Heart gives a quarter to a beggar. The sky
is azure blue. He has neither schedules, nor obligations.
There's nothing he need do. Ought Heart ponder what
he's found out? Thought-bites apropos postponed profits
and prevailing pleasures? Instead, he searches the yard
for a four leaf clover: a good-luck wish to save for later.

THE MINUTE GRIT IN
DEATH'S UNDERGARMENTS

Each fuck is a poke in Death's meddlesome eye.
So thinks Heart. You know how airports once used
a revolving light to peek beneath your shades at night?
Like this does Death survey the mortal landscape.
But a poke, you protest, surely Heart exaggerates.
Okay, let's try again. You have seen how thousands of
moths, gnats, innumerable unnamable bugs will flit
against a street light, so does the domain of fucking
seek to vex the gyrations of Death's nosy instrument
of vision, the very searchlight of Heart's imagination.
So each fuck, Heart repeats, is a poke in Death's eye,
even if it's a bantam nudge, clearly minuscule, almost
non-existent. Sex for Heart is many things and love,
too, is surely Death's particular irritant, the constant
chafe of minute grit in Death's dark undergarments.
Likewise intimacy, the wish for a hug to be so close
that all the space between, the pockets of solitude,
are decisively erased. Moreover, each fuck is a variety
of talk for which words are incomplete, so an example,
in potential, resembles two philosophies intermeshed:
shuffle, shuffle, like two sex-starved decks of cards.
Heart could write a book on the metaphysically nutritive
value of sex and even its worth as basic exercise in that
sex makes the heart beat fast and extends one's vitality,
mortality, even biography. Death abhors the very idea
of salutary exertion—see how eagerly it pops the heart

of some libidinous old galoot wheezing toward climax.
Death hates fucking, it's as simple as that. Oh, Heart
has it figured out. This is his area of special expertise.
And so, after all the other rationalizing has been done,
after the kisses, the fondlings, and sweet exchanges,
when Heart comes to rest with legs entwined in post-
coital bliss, he exults to see Death stagger away holding
one skeletal paw to his eye or perhaps its bony socket.
Ouch, Death bawls, as he searches for a remnant pool
of tears left over from funeral or recent tragedy to soothe
his orb: Death's own eye, of course, being forever dry.

MacFleckna's Storefront Church

Heart has grown enamored of a pear-shaped critic,
the Boss Tweed of poetry's Tammany Hall, whose
blackthorn eyes and enduring curves arouse in him
the ambition to be authenticated in Latinate rhetoric.
Oh, MacFleckna, Heart cries out, teach me what love
is all about! Heart's life is language, even the writing
of parking tickets and bistro menus excites the ruckus
within his chest; but what thrills him most are epistles
of amour, billet doux from him to you, be they verse
or hieroglyphics cut in granite, since Heart's gift exists
as tone and topic, which is part of his current problem.
You see, while each bit of Heart's flung spit is diction,
he himself is dying meat and will in due time *de*compose.
Heart yearns for transubstantiation, to turn his physique
to vast articulation, just as flesh and blood in a contrary
communion can be changed to bread and wine. Hasn't
Heart often said the world exists to wind up in a book?
He knows he wrote that someplace and if his lady wrote
a book on Heart, then not only would his life be words,
then he would be words as well. He'd be composed of print
while composing print himself. Can any writer profess
to exist before a critic has cast that writer into speech?
Life as text with Heaven in the library stacks—no doubt
a step up from crypt or vault. Such is Heart's ambition.
To begin, he arranges bouquets of pens on MacFleckna's
front stoop, reams of paper on which she may record

happy thoughts about Heart. Unluckily, the lady has no
interest in our hero. He remains for her an unruly cipher.
It's pure mind she's after or at least its resemblance:
The luster of meaning without the burden of meaning.
So when Heart submits his work, she returns it stamped
rejected. This reduces Heart's life to the level of a beast's,
since, like a beast, he will possess no life beyond the tomb.
Worse, in this time of disbelief, only critics may bequeath
life everlasting until each becomes a tweed bedecked Jesus,
teasing poets with the hope of a spot in kingdom come.
MacFleckna, cries Heart, grant me the gift of eternal life!
In what church may your genius be praised? Is it ghetto
storefront or gothic cathedral? Then he hits upon a strategy.
The subject of Heart's verse will be MacFleckna herself,
her brains, beauty, and pushy nature. Each word by Heart
will be a concrete block in the Statue of Libertylike statue
of MacFleckna, dearest, deathless critic. Won't she glorify
Heart's intellect in order to be turned into language herself?
Thus MacFleckna will immortalize them both. Arm in arm
they'll roam among the spectral forms of Dickinson and Yeats.
Confidently, Heart prepares to pitch his tent before the portals
of his paramour's critical acumen with his clutch of verse
and beggar's cup. Oh, MacFleckna, he'll cry out, splay yourself
vast and rampant to my ardent touch! Hardly will his words
fade on the air then he'll hear the antique gates groan open
on their rusty hinges, widening with a lusty cry reminiscent
of a virgin's first night among the riffraff of sexual abandon.

THEIR TÊTE-À-TÊTE IS DONE

Something deep, resembling headache or plantar wart—
Heart is struck by how grief operates beneath the level
of thought, like a river flowing from Ohio to Tennessee
yet skipping Kentucky completely by going underneath.
But at times, thinks Heart, there must be swampy ground
as water percolates up to the surface to replace dry land
so that on bad days Farmer Brown's cows are muddy
right to their ear tips. Such is Heart's kinship to grief
since Woody's death—grief's black river has bubbled
to the top and Heart finds his progress slow as he slogs
through muck; i.e., dirt made soft by the addition of woe.
Heart of course would prefer to be happy but the option
has been taken from him. It feels as if his mind were blank,
yet within him hunkers grief, as if Heart weren't thinking
but was being thought. As if all the emotions—joy, pride,
envy, and the rest—had their sturdy engines among the stars
that kept them going, but they needed a vehicle on earth.
So Heart and humanity were brought forth. That's our job,
thinks Heart, to form a screen upon which the emotions
can perform and today grief gets to skip across the boards.
And although Heart knows that Woody is six feet under,
today he's slow on the uptake because ten times he's gone
to the phone to give Woody a buzz or wondered what's new
in Woody's life or recalled a joke that Woody might like
while in fact Woody's no more than a fresh supply of slops
on the grim reaper's worm farm, making each of Heart's
retrospections a mini-enactment of Woody's leave-taking,
meaning his friend croaks not just once but each time Heart

concocts a wisecrack for his pal. That's death's big flaw,
decides Heart, it's not final. It creeps along until one's own.
Worse, it gives the dead the last word in any discourse, chat,
or quarrel so that if Heart were to say, Just think or What about . . . ,
only a drone would emerge from the other end of the phone.
Their tête-à-tête is done, leading Heart to brood about words
not said, kisses ungiven, upping the ante of sorrow's burden.
So Heart records a tape on which he sings his favorite songs,
tells a joke about a dog, and inserts the exact amount of Heart
data his friends need before they quit this earth. To play the tape
takes all day. Do his chums listen? Perhaps for five minutes. So he
rents a sound truck and at three A.M. as Maria, John, and Harry
pile pillows on their heads, speakers on the street blare out,
I love you X and think you smart. This being Heart's attempt
to lessen future grief. Yet won't it give him further reason to regret?
Not that he'll drive his friends to sudden expiration from sleep
deprivation, but Heart begins to get rude notes from his pals
saying how they are his pals no longer. This too is a solution:
no friends, no grief. But for Heart it's too reckless a decision.
Instead, he contents himself with staring into his friends' eyes
longingly, as if to stockpile brain cells jammed with memory,
until a friend asks: What makes you think I'll die before you?
which startles Heart who knows that Death strikes down other folks
but could it happen to him as well? Me, too? he asks. No doubt
it would be a first. And like a vision comes the image of himself
tottering along the brink of the white space spilling past this point.

DEATH LOBS A BOSOM
INTO THE FIELD

Toys that bounce, toys that jingle, toys that go whizbang—
Heart loves his playthings even when he does not play.
He loves the value of nullity, the delicacy of frivolity.
The stuffed bears of early childhood—he would put them
in a church in which the god of jokes was praised. The ghosts
of a million games beset him still. The flying catch he made
when he was eight, the miniature tank that could drag a cat—
walking or eating a snack, Heart's mind will be overswept
by recollection and he will laugh. This permits Heart to advance.
Gravity enabled by buoyancy—like the country bisected
by the Mississippi: toys on one side, seriousness on the other.
Doesn't Charlie Chaplin make Ronald Reagan tolerable?
For Heart, it's the fragility of toys that makes them work—
soap bubbles and balsam gliders—just as the flower's beauty
is increased by the brevity of its life, or else it becomes a weed.
So let's say Heart's friends have flown to Texas, his toilet
breaks, and he owes a packet on his taxes: the fact of a joke,
paper kite, game of chess, even the modest Whoopee cushion
exist as weights to set upon the balance, which lets sadness rise
and gloom disperse. Does it work? Not always, but the idea,
thinks Heart, is sound. This gives the lie to those who claim
that Heart's embrace of nonsense suggests a silly nature. Quite
the reverse. Only by the ridiculous can death be calibrated.
Only by carnage can we appreciate the giddiness of laughter.
Else why bother? Thus Heart becomes thinker extraordinaire.
As a student of the conflicting magnetic fields of sentiment,

Heart deduces that forward motion is the result of momentum
stemming from the collision of opposites. Not that Heart
has it so neatly figured out. Instead he sees himself engaged
in a special game of fetch: Death has for each of us on earth
a chosen ball. For Heart it's a single breast, delicate contours,
doubloon-shaped aureole, chipper nipple, and, in harmony
with Heart's love of diversity, neither age, color, nor religion
bear any weight. Death lobs the bosom into a field and Heart
goes running after. Dutifully, he brings it back and drops it
at Death's feet. This is, for Heart, his toy and he could run all day.
But each time Death flings it out, he flings it a trifle further;
and, although eager, Heart gets each time a trifle more fatigued.
The fields are green, the flowers bloom. This is, for Heart, a life,
with all life's shiny oxymorons, each day's paradoxes of breath.
But in time the shadows lengthen as Heart gets ready to depart.
A night bird trills, a bell chimes, cows shuffle back to the barn.

DAYTONA FRESH
AND INDIANAPOLIS
IMMACULATE

Just as a long rainy night in winter softens the trees,
so is Heart softened by time. And just as the toenails
of Heart's big toes, snoutlike in their own left or right,
increasingly with the passing years imitate concrete,
so is the world ossified by time's prolongation, or so
it seems to Heart. While I thaw, he thinks, the world
beyond me solidifies. There exists to this a symmetry
which Heart gets but does not like. This is the reason
as Heart grows older he takes his lovers from women
of an equal ripeness. No kids for Heart. The diamond
facets of their green and callow nakedness would rival
glass fragments against the fragile chamois of his belly.
What's the point? Soft likes soft, it's as simple as that.
So Heart seeks ladies who share his debility, although
this forms a mental insight only, since, paradoxically,
his senses tell him differently. For example: as time's
corrugations continue to sculpt the face of his beloved,
Heart's eyeballs become further enfeebled, which keeps
the potholed street of his dearest's chin, brow, and cheek
Daytona fresh and Indianapolis immaculate. Likewise,
as her smoke- and whiskey-sifted voice snaps and crackles
with advancing prime, so the fenestra vestibulae of Heart's
middle ear pulls down its shade, his tympanic membrane

begins to molder, which sweetens his sweetheart's cacophony
to a wrenlike warble till her squawking turns to dulcet song.
Isn't this true of each person's progress toward the tomb?
As life's sense stimuli peak, one's sense receivers dull,
which is why Heart considers encrusting his lover's breasts
with red pepper or adding a dash of vinegar or skunk smut
to her Chanel or Shalimar. For Heart, thanks to the decline
of his sensory apparatus, his fragility marches in lockstep
with their pliancy and his lady friends stay forever young.
As both lose their teeth, their kisses grow more velveteen.
As the crick in Heart's prick increasingly duplicates a U-turn,
so the welcoming nethernest of his ladylove keeps widening.
And won't this persist? As each sense like a succulent grape
is plucked from the aging body, so the idea that something
is missing is erased. As the skeleton shrinks and outer flesh
of lover and beloved depicts the pulp of an overripe peach,
so the body of each forms the protective buffer of the other,
until Heart's heartthrob begins to resemble the football pads
he wore in his youth, while he himself apes the moon-shaped
rubber cups his sweetling once packed deep into her brassiere
or the wadding she tacked to buttock or shoulder, except today
those falsies will be Heart. Now that Heart understands life's
terminal drift, he'll never abandon his final helpmate in death
but plans to share her coffin or to make a place for her in his,
so that stretched out side by side they might putrefy together;
and as they decompose, each will come to compose the other,
joined in one arena of flesh as both player and playing field
combined; and when that flesh is gone and what's left is bone,
they will be closer yet, with their skulls clicked in combination
like low balls in Death's fell billiard game or the double O's
in *foot* or *boot*. Here aging stops and they return to their roots—

rib bones intertwined like teenage lovers holding hands—
as their souls' closest coupling is kept for last and the two
become one dollop of mush, one heap of chips, one dust.

For Thomas Lux

WHEN TUBES PIERCE EVERY EXTREMITY

Wrinkled face and liver-spotted hands,
Heart is struck by how the apparatus
of living descends toward disintegration,
while looking outward remains fresh and
antique free with each article he looks at
neither old nor gray. True, he needs glasses
and cataracts may glaze his orbs with ash,
but the unhindered act of vision contains
no temporal burden, the objects of his sight
neither reveal nor reflect his mortal passing,
unless nearby mirror or shop window hurls
his reflection back, a boomerang to smack
Heart right between the eyes. Sitting in a chair,
examining the room, he could in fact be young.
This is not a sort of wishful thinking as Heart
is seriously perplexed. For instance, in the park
where he strolls after lunch he views the swings
with all but eager pleasure and isn't this a danger
since Heart is long past the age when he is able
to swing by his heels? What's more, he feels equal
in age to everybody younger than he, descending
to the age of three, while his true contemporaries
appear obsolete, until Heart must grab his lapels
and shout, That's me! Heart had enough obstacles
in youth to have no wish to repeat, and yet the grass
looks just as green, the girls as cute, and so Heart

fears that he might slip. But peering in the mirror
past beard and wrinkles, Heart sees that his organs
of sight bear no sign of aging. They suffer neither
balding, nor fatigue. Heart's eyes are wrinkle-free,
as if they'd never aged. As a result, each object
he sees seems new and even, in illusion, Heart, too.
This fabrication must be the wellspring of hope,
since if Heart truly saw his life through the filter
of what he had lived, he'd never crawl from bed.
And so his eyes play tricks and retain their wonder,
look as young as ever, which allows the looker
(in this case Heart) also to look young, although
in fancy only. How shrewd is Heart's machinery
to keep him going past all meaning, so even when
he reaches a century and has thick tubes running
into each enfeebled extremity, his wrinkle-proof orbs—
as glossy as ever—will fix on the white-sheathed
butt of an unsuspecting nurse. Why not, he'll think,
don't we strut our lumps on time's identical stage?
And out creeps the old joy-hook for a fortifying pinch.

For L.G.

THE MORGUE ATTENDANTS
CLUTCH THEIR KEYS

Heart checks out the morgue at midnight to catch
the dead in the midst of their tricks. He had thought
to find them lounging side by side on marble slabs
as in antique mezzotints. Instead each corpse has
a private refrigerator, thus ensuring that his or her
unconditional loneliness begins before the tomb.
Heart kneels down beside one stainless steel door.
From inside he detects a whistling. *My daddy was
an engineer,* runs the song. It's one of Heart's favorites.
My sister balled the jack, whistles Heart in response.
From another locker comes a weeping, from a third
mordant laughter. The lockers look like horizontal
toilet stalls where unknown but nonunique activities
occur behind closed doors. Except here the occupants
are stuck—motor skills being kaput—so Heart decides
to let them out and wheels the dead into the room.
The corpses are stretched flat beneath white sheets
which Heart folds back to expose the head of each.
You've seen how people dreaming move their eyes
behind closed lids? Ditto the recent dead, but more
slowly as their memories fade. Soon Heart has them
lined up in a row, men on the right, ladies on the left.
He goes to each and pats a hand, smoothes a brow.
Any secrets? Heart asks. Any last requests? But freed
from their freezer chests each corpse in this fugitive
hiatus between fleeting life and abiding death can only

make a single sound: the exhalation of trapped gases,
an intonation located between a squeezebox and a sigh.
The ladies make high notes, the men's run from tenor
to bass. Dreary, you might think, but Heart can tell
they like it. After all, though slight, it's all that's left
of self-expression. Likewise, they are happy to be
en masse instead of solo in his or her refrigerator.
But let's move past this transitional period as Heart
works out the kinks. As dawn breaks, he's grouped
the corpses in a chorus with each cadaver responsible
for a single wheezing note. They try many melodies
before returning to the tune that Heart heard when
he first came. *My brother drove a hack,* the dead sing out—
a bagpipe expiration, a casting off of remnant memory.
My mother took in laundry. Heart perches on a chair,
his hair tossed like Toscanini as he calls up the notes
with a pointed finger—high C here, A-flat there—
starting over at the end and each time a little louder.
Outside, the morning shift of morgue attendants
hover and clutch their keys, disinclined to enter.
I'll never be done with my wandering, drone the dead,
never done with wandering. Out on the street, buses take
the living to work as day number XXX cranks up.

LAST JUMPING JACKS

Heart deliberates upon the end of the world.
Will there be fireworks or universal gloom?
Flash flood or plague—anything could happen.
Even a rogue asteroid. He imagines the streets
with everyone gone. No more standing in line
at the butcher's, parking places readily available.
But what will Judgment Day be like? A gnashing
of teeth, singing of hymns? He considers the Matterhorn
of deeds people will wish to have completed sooner—
not bills paid or the roof fixed, but the embraces
they let go to waste, kisses ungiven or unforgiven.
And wouldn't they fill a library—those sentences
bemoaned or left unsaid? Apologies, tributes, even
insults just a jiffy too late. Oh, five minutes more,
beg the multitudes as they're pushed out the door.
Heart imagines waking on the last day and hearing
the bad news: the world will stop at three o'clock.
Would he resume smoking? Would he swig whiskey?
He imagines the sky an odd yellow color. The birds
are silent, shops empty—what remains to be bought?
He imagines his neighbors on their front porches—
a few scratching their heads, a few wiping their eyes.
Heart will make his bed, scrub the last night's dishes.
He'll call a few friends, listen to Schubert or Monk.
For an hour he will write in his diary. After lunch
he takes the dog for a walk. The sky remains yellow;
the air has grown still. He does his jumping jacks,

then he waters the garden, takes out the trash. This,
of course, is what Heart hopes, but whatever the case
when the world quits at last, he'll be like a light bulb
before the power is cut—still burning, still bright.

THE WORLD'S SIDEWALKS
AND DAILY HOOPLA

When Heart's lover's breast gets lopped off—a surgeon's rejoinder to cancer's inroads—Heart asks if his kisses, too, have been excised. Not that his lover—by now an ex—has any use for Heart's inquiry, and Heart as well grasps the triviality of his concern. Still, if with a hundred kisses, like a coat of paint, his lover's breast he once bedecked, then this breast had a thickness of kisses equal to breast itself and this day equally decreased. Does Heart mourn? There on breast rubbish heap breast and ancient caresses lie entwined. But what Heart mourns most is duration's indifferent passage and how his own blissful ignorance falls victim to time's education, for as he was spreading his kisses on her bosom like margarine on a bun not once did the possible breach of chest and breast occur to him. For this Heart remains grateful but it makes him solemn and leads him to tote up those prior partners from whom bits and pieces have been excised or who have themselves fallen away from the world's sidewalks and daily hoopla. Likewise Heart thinks how time checks back to scrape its muddy feet on what was becoming pristine memory as Heart gradually forgot the lesser details—limp dick, bug bites, crick in back, which had rendered the original occasion merely human, two creatures banging together in desperation before returning to their existential stalls. In fact, just as memory with a complete lack of reflection was blooming into legend, Heart heard the news—breast

flipped to garbage heap and now kaput—and with it came
the worry that all the dazzling narratives which had kindled
the stained glass windows of his body's church were equally
suspect, hyperbolized recitals of brief trysts with long gone
body parts, the rubbing together of flesh which with time
has become either concertinalike or defunct—so much ash
or compost to help a meager posy heavenward, albeit briefly.
And me too, thinks Heart, for, though never a prize, inch
by inch he slides toward the boobihood of age; so it's not
that women avoid his glance, they don't even distinguish
his passage—seeing as forgettable what Heart once saw as vast.
In escape Heart turns his mind to those flinching primitives,
how each group put its particular map upon the Rorschach
of night sky—there a bear, a little further a fallen warrior.
Solo in his backyard at night Heart cranes his neck to seek
the former recipients of his ardent kisses in the firmament's
black and speckled melon-half, as the summer's cicadas jazz
in parody of Heart's bygone passion—surely those six stars
to the north depict a nearly forgotten pair of lips; and that
triangular constellation above the oak, see how the darkness
it encloses echoes a sweet departed's nether thatch; and look,
that curve of stars to the south, no doubt they form in outline
the excised breast that gave rise to Heart's current cogitation—
and his breathing quickens as he unveils again the downward
slope, the arched expanse of velvet skin, the perky nipple.

ACKNOWLEDGMENTS

Acknowledgments are due to the editors of the following publications, in whose pages some of the poems in this book first appeared.

The American Poetry Review: "Oh, Immobility, Death's Vast Associate"

The Clackamas Review: "Great Job," "Old What's His Name," "One Good Turn Deserves Another"

The Gettysburg Review: "No Tangos Tonight," "Last Jumping Jacks"

The Harvard Review: "Can Poetry Matter?" "Flawed Language: Thought's Shadow," "Occupant In Permanent Transit," "The World's Sidewalks And Daily Hoopla," "What Good Is Love Unless It's Aggressive?" "Wounds Without Pain"

The Marlboro Review: "The Dark And Turbulent Sea," "Death Lobs A Bosom Into The Field"

Ploughshares: "Like A Revolving Door," "Thus He Endured"

Poetry: "His Favorite Blue Cup," "Why Fool Around," "The Minute Grit In Death's Undergarments"

Salmagundi: "Until We Drool And Piss Ourselves"

The Virginia Quarterly Review: "Facing Failure," "The New Austerity"

ABOUT THE AUTHOR

Stephen Dobyns is the author of nine prior books of poetry and twenty novels, including ten mystery novels set in Saratoga Springs. His collection of essays on poetry, *Best Words, Best Order* was published in 1996. His first book of poems, *Concurring Beasts,* was the Lamont Poetry Selection of 1971. *Black Dog, Red Dog* was a winner of the 1984 National Poetry Series competition. *Cemetery Nights* was chosen for the Poetry Society of America's Melville Cane Award in 1987. Dobyns has received a Guggenheim Fellowship for his poetry and three fellowships from the National Endowment of the Arts. His most recent book of poetry is *Common Carnage* (1996). His most recent novel is *Boy in the Water* (1999). Dobyns lives with his family near Boston.

PENGUIN POETS